Bob Marley and Media

POPULAR MUSICS MATTER: SOCIAL, POLITICAL AND CULTURAL INTERVENTIONS

Series Editors: Eoin Devereux, Aileen Dillane and Martin J. Power

The Popular Musics Matter: Social, Political and Cultural Interventions series will publish internationally informed edited collections, monographs and textbooks that engage in the critical study of popular music performance (live and recorded), historical and contemporary popular music practitioners and artists, and participants and audiences for whom such musics embody aesthetic, cultural, and, particularly, socio-political values. The series sees music not only as a manifestation of global popular culture but also as a form that profoundly shapes and continually seeks to redefine our understandings of how society operates in a given location and era.

Titles in the Series

Soundtracking Germany: Popular Music and National Identity, Melanie Schiller
Heart and Soul: Critical Essays on Joy Division, edited by Eoin Devereux, Martin J. Power and Aileen Dillane
Deindustrialisation and Popular Music: Punk and 'Post-Punk' in Manchester, Düsseldorf, Torino and Tampere, Giacomo Bottà
Bob Marley and Media: Representation and Audiences, Mike Hajimichael

Bob Marley and Media

Representation and Audiences

Mike Hajimichael

ROWMAN & LITTLEFIELD
Lanham • Boulder • New York • London

Published by Rowman & Littlefield
An imprint of The Rowman & Littlefield Publishing Group, Inc.
4501 Forbes Boulevard, Suite 200, Lanham, Maryland 20706
www.rowman.com

86-90 Paul Street, London EC2A 4NE

Copyright © 2023 by The Rowman & Littlefield Publishing Group, Inc.

All rights reserved. No part of this book may be reproduced in any form or by any electronic or mechanical means, including information storage and retrieval systems, without written permission from the publisher, except by a reviewer who may quote passages in a review.

British Library Cataloguing in Publication Information Available

Library of Congress Cataloging-in-Publication Data

Names: Hajimichael, Michael, author.
Title: Bob Marley and media : representation and audiences / Mike Hajimichael.
Description: Lanham : Rowman & Littlefield, 2023. | Series: Popular musics matter: social, political, and cultural interventions | Includes bibliographical references and index.
Identifiers: LCCN 2022046328 (print) | LCCN 2022046329 (ebook) | ISBN 9781538165454 (cloth) | ISBN 9798881806569 (pbk) | ISBN 9781538165461 (ebook)
Subjects: LCSH: Marley, Bob—In mass media. | Marley, Bob—Appreciation. | Reggae music—Political aspects.
Classification: LCC ML420.M3313 H37 2023 (print) | LCC ML420.M3313 (ebook) | DDC 782.421646092--dc23/eng/20220930
LC record available at https://lccn.loc.gov/2022046328
LC ebook record available at https://lccn.loc.gov/2022046329

∞™ The paper used in this publication meets the minimum requirements of American National Standard for Information Sciences—Permanence of Paper for Printed Library Materials, ANSI/NISO Z39.48-1992.

To Bob . . . if only some people understood. . . .

Contents

Acknowledgments		ix
Verse One	In this great future, you can't forget your past . . .	1
Verse Two	Too Much Mix Up, Mix Up	9
Verse Three	Radio Waves Limiting the Gong	23
Verse Four	What the Papers Say	43
Verse Five	The Revolution That Was Not Televised	65
Verse Six	Duppy Conqueror – Life After Death	87
Verse Seven	Won't You Help Me Sing . . .	103
Bibliography		109
Index		127
About the Author		131

Acknowledgments

Writing this book has been like taking a long journey over a number of years. Most books start from somewhere. I thank Jah Hammer Sound System from Ipswich, Britain who in 1981 carried the sad news – live and direct – that Bob Marley had passed away. . . . Many years later a conversation in a pub in Limerick, with Martin J. Power and Aileen Dillane, led me to start thinking about this journey some more. I thank both of them for their encouragement to 'go for it'. A big thanks to Mike Alleyne who gave me space to initially share some of these ideas about Marley and radio (2019) and that took things to a different level. Getting more practical, developing ideas and formal proposals to publishers I started to get the wheels turning. For that process I am deeply indebted to my long-time friend and comrade Michael Mullen for his wise thoughts and critical eye. To my surprise some publishers responded that Bob Marley was not 'mainstream enough'. With 25,000,000 copies of *Legend* (Marley 1984) sold, I still find those views hard to digest (Schaal 2021). Fortunately, in life you connect with some wonderfully positive-minded people. Rebecca Anastasi then at Rowman & Littlefield Publishers backed the idea and guided me through the proposal process and review and finally a contract appeared. Meantime of course, research data collection commenced. Rebecca has moved on now, and Michael Tan then took over as my contact. I would like to thank him for answering all my emails giving crucial advice. A special salute also goes to my long-time friend and bredren Versioncos/Costantinos Pissourios for the beautiful interpretation of my ideas as an illustration on the front cover of this book. There are very few people in the world with as much knowledge on Bob Marley than 'sensei' Roger Steffens who provided a wealth of information and valuable time to talk. I am humbled by Roger's wisdom and constant feedback – give thanks RasRojah. Dennis Howard, my bredren and fellow academic at the University of West Indies provided crucial insight and advice – especially about the jukebox theory-Respect. In the writing and research phases, many people provided their support and I really value their time and effort. Big thanks to my son Giorgio, for his astute eye for detail and feedback with various drafts and computer fixing. Anna Millans for Spanish translations and Dionysia Dionysiou for administrative and research support. I would also like to thank so many people for the wisdom and time to do interviews and answer my emails, particularly John Tobler, Bingie Barker, Paul Gambaccini, Tony Brown, Harare Dread, Joe Jergunsen, Paul Bradshaw, and Lepki Rebel (RiP) and Mike Williams from DBC. A heartfelt thanks also goes out to John Solomos for passing on the knowledge that patience is the key, along with being humble. Additionally, a big salute to my work colleague Nicos Trimikliniotis for the guidance and inspiration to write on. In the final phases, when the pressure got hot, thanks to the media folks I collaborated with whoever gave some time out to get things over the line. Bigup Mark @ Niceup Radio, Dennis @ Riddim1Radio, Dimi, my Blues Brother @ Radio Blind Dog (our regular chats on air about the book's progress helped me focus so much) and Steve @ UKVibe. My deepest gratitude goes to Marina and Melina, the rest of my family, for putting up with lengthy absences 'writing a book in the room' and my brothers, Perry and George, who I can now visit more regularly. Finally, a big thanks to my friend Charlie Shekeris for his philosophical insights in solving a troubling citation.

Verse One

In this great future, you can't forget your past . . .

One line by Bob Marley from the well-known song 'No Woman No Cry' (Marley 1975b) serves as a reminder of the necessity to take into account how the singer was portrayed in the past by the media to different audiences throughout the world. The main goals of this book are to revise media content by comprehending these representations and to look for illuminating information in media texts that may have passed us by. Before going into more depth about this, I would like to share a personal experience that in many ways influenced my interest in Bob Marley. Evening, 11 May 1981. Entering the events room, a sonic boom permeated through my bones. Reggae sound systems always had that effect, with a deep bass from a wall of speakers stacked up to the ceiling with the DJ's voice wailing over the sound 'Bob Marley dead and gone, but his memory lives on'. This is how I found out Bob Marley had died—through a sound system from Ipswich called Jah Hammer Hi-Fi in Colchester, at Essex University, in a function room behind the Student Union Bar. Ever since then, the sound system has been an important part of my life. There was something crucial that this sad news came through the medium. It felt so unfiltered, real, and raw.

In days to come, the news travelled through different media, such as television, radio, newspapers and magazines. It was processed, manufactured, canned like a tin of baked beans. Back then, pre-internet, news did not travel at an instant. More or less though, the same day of his death, the news spread across the world's different time zones.

The MC's voice wailed the same phrase, over and over, adding lines like 'you hear it on the radio, see it on the TV show, read it in the paper, everywhere you walk and go—Bob Marley dead and gone'. Looking back on it, on this day, Bob Marley was everywhere. Somehow, for most of the last decade, when he was touring the world, from my observation as a fan, he featured rarely on mainstream media. Maybe a lip-syncing appearance on *Top of the Pops*, but he was not the conventional 'everywhere' type of pop star. The only time I recalled hearing his voice was in an interview with David Rodigan, on Capital Radio in the summer of 1980. Little did I know that some forty years later, I would be listening to it again, transcribing every word for this publication. The audio cassette of that interview became worn out with time from too much usage. The point is that during the 1970s, mainstream media did not represent reggae, and it did not even represent Bob Marley, and this stayed in my mind as a problematic issue. Decades later, as I reflect back on this, I wander through my thoughts on how to start to explain 'Bob Marley and Media' and the points of inspiration for its creation. Certainly that moment in time in 1981 played a part in laying a kind of conceptual foundation stone, in that the authenticity of sound system as a form of media, carrying the news, influenced many aspects of my life, as a musician, poet, MC, and academic writing on this form of a popular music. Beyond that, my drive to write this book stems from two key themes.

One is easy to argue, and as I will show in Verse Two, there is not enough academic writing on Bob Marley. Most of the existing literature is often biographic and reminiscent of a compost heap, where writers simply regurgitate what came before them. Additionally, the main inspiration for this book is that there is no evidence of rigorous research on the subject of Bob Marley and media, particularly during the period he was most active internationally, 1972–1980. Specifically, my interest is how Marley was represented, through which media, from radio to printed press and television. This was not inspired by any sense of conspiracy but simply out of a curiosity to review and take in as much media content on the subject matter when the artist was at the height of his career. Subsequent to this I was also curious to explore what happened musically after Marley died on 11 May 1981. The death of Marley is very similar to that of other famous pop stars, such as Elvis (1977), John Lennon (1980), Michael Jackson (2009), Amy Winehouse (2011), Whitney Houston (2012), David Bowie (2016), Prince (2016) and George Michael (2016).[1] Making meaning of the way 'stars keep shining' is complicated due to the polysemic character of how their 'after life' is manufactured and negotiated by a range of people from family, musicians they worked with in bands, to record companies that own their artistic works, the media in all its forms and, last, but by no means least, fans. In the context of Bob Marley, as we will see in Verse Six, this afterlife resulted in his deification and apotheosis, as well as his fame and money reaching entirely unparalleled levels of commodification and hyperactivity.

Taking this journey through vast amounts of media texts was not an easy process, but in some ways I counted myself lucky. Had I begun this type of book say, thirty years ago, analysing media would have required physical presence—going through archives in a variety of places, making photocopies, analysing and then reviewing content. Data is primarily at our fingertips in the digital age, and this makes the job of doing a book on media content somewhat easier. I would also add that this data exists in a variety of forms such as discography, tour schedule, dedicated web sites, videos, photographic content, all of which contribute to telling a variety of stories.[2] At the same time, it is critical to highlight some limitations. Due to lack of availability and access, it was impossible to include every media interview and print article on Bob Marley. Nonetheless, I believe we have sufficient qualitative and narrative material to think about based on the data collected.

Before presenting a brief synopsis of the book's structure, I would like to elaborate a little bit on issues of methodology, exploratory research, and understanding key words such as representation, texts and audiences.

Exploratory research might sound like a mission in the applied sciences and often its inductive approach is dismissed as unscientific (McAleese and Kilty 2019). One of the problems with such a dismissive approach to qualitative research is it is often evaluated through quantitative perspectives. The relevance of how many times a specific narrative occurs in collecting data is not as significant as the content of the narrative. I will explain this across the entirety of this book, as media content in a variety of forms struck me in aspects of what was conveyed, how and by whom—which leads us to consider two key words in the title of this book, 'representation' and 'audiences'. Representation with regard to media content is an important issue in my academic research, starting from a PhD at The Centre for Contemporary Cultural Studies that concerned the ways in which Cyprus and Cypriots had been represented in a variety of textual forms (Hajimichael 1995). Representation in the media refers to how media such as television, film, radio, and the printed press portray particular groups of people or communities but this approach should never be taken too literally because representation is also 'constitutive' (Hall 1997). Meaning itself is open to interpretation by audiences; consequently, it is often contested because people in audiences interpret content differently. Although media producers sometimes attempt to fix meaning in a particular way with stereotypes, the idea that all representation is fixed is flawed (Hall 1997). A lot of Hall's media-based research devoted itself to exposing and deconstructing how ideology shaped media messages. He illustrated the media's role in advancing certain narratives and meanings, while silencing or marginalising others and thereby constructing understandings of reality in particular ways (Hall 1997).

In this context, because audiences are diverse and complex, contrary to what marketing department managers and social media influencers may tell us, media frequently reflect or are directed toward different audiences. This book is an attempt to comprehend the variety of media portrayals of Bob Marley. We will look at how media reflected different audiences and contexts, and how they ultimately shaped our understanding of the singer through media discourses. I am particularly interested in finding out what these representations constitute and how influential they were in the formation of ideas on Marley.

This type of research is also distinctive and grounded because it entails investigating texts that we often take for granted or have not been revised from the past, such as music press articles, radio interviews, and television programs. Much of my research and writing to date has this exploratory characteristic, such as study on Thomson, who was the first British colonial photographer in Cyprus (2006), the uniqueness of online music production (2011), the first and only vinyl record label in Cyprus (2015), and the power of social memes as fake news discourses on refugees (2021a). This method of research engagement represents a calling and a challenge for me. The relative lack of substantial academic writing on Bob Marley presented me with my greatest academic challenge to date. This is largely due to the volume of data and the fact that when I began writing this book roughly three years ago, no one had ever written a comprehensive and analytical treatment of the subject in terms of media content. Therefore, how the media reported, reflected, and spoke about Marley is a continuation of an academic path that I have chosen to follow, grounded in data and information that has been largely unexplored previously. When I began exploring the data collected for this book, I had a hunch that adopting a single method of analysis for such a diverse range of content, radio, television, printed texts, and websites, would be flawed due to the variety of media platforms, contexts and texts. I decided to have a flexible approach based on applying methods that seemed appropriate for the different content collected. Radio content required a lot of background research on context and sensitivities on different types of radio grounded from the data. For television and video content, a similar approach was adopted, combined with narrative and a close analysis of content with regard to representation and ideology (Hall 1997), whereas the volume of printed texts from magazines and newspapers facilitated the application of in-depth document analysis (Bowen 2009). The key element that binds these methods together is that findings are based on the collected data, which means that my analysis employs a bottom-up strategy to collect, investigate, and analyse what the media had to say about Bob Marley.

I quickly realised two things during my research. Firstly, different forms of media present information differently, necessitating distinct research methodologies. Media vary in what they do and to what extent, and within each medium, there are a variety of representations due to the different audiences they targeted and their format and style. As will be explained in Verse Four, a feature in *Playboy* magazine is radically different from the music and entertainment magazine *Swing* in Jamaica, for example. Being interviewed for a college campus radio station is radically different from being interviewed for BBC Radio largely because these media appeal to different audiences and operate radically differently. A lot of this relates to fundamental insights in relation to popular music and meaning, which differs based on what, who, and how meaning is conveyed (Longhurst 2014, 23). Additionally, there is a tendency for current research to be fascinated with all things digital and 'new' and media analysis has become synonymous with 'social media analysis'. While some of the content in Verse Six refers to data on Marley from platforms such as Twitter, Facebook, and TikTok, most of my analysis concerns more traditional media forms during a specifically defined time period. While this might be seen as nostalgic, I believe, with too much emphasis on social media research, there is a tendency to underestimate 'traditional' media's importance culturally, historically, and politically.

Regarding the structure of the book, I would like it to be taken as Verses symbolically represented as tracks on two sides of a vinyl record, on distinct themes which have linkages. My inspiration for this approach comes from a great dub release from 'The Mighty Zulu Warrior' Jah Shaka (1982) who named tracks as different verses on the same theme. These sometimes vary in length, like all good releases, and there is a reprise at the end that amalgamates some reflections on the whole body of work. I present all of this as food for thought, grounded in a wide range of media texts.

Verse Two explores existing works on Bob Marley as a mix-up of categories and ideas. While this is not a book, in a biographical sense, about Bob Marley, I felt the need to review a variety of existing literature on the subject matter for the sake of being more rooted on the topic. As we will see, the majority of work, which is biographic, came out after the death of the singer in 1981 (White 1983; Davis 1983). Scholarly works are also considered by a number of authors (Alleyne 1994, 2000, 2019a; Gilroy 2005; Stephens 1998 and Toynbee 2007). These, as we shall see, are diverse and contrasting in their reasoned approaches. Some works as I shall show, written by more seasoned media practitioners fit somewhere between 'biography' and more scholarly grounded ethnographic work (Goldman 2006; Steffens 2018b). Additionally, there are biographies written by immediate family members (Marley and Jones 2005; Marley and Winkler 2015). These give a different insight that even challenges some of the mythologizing of earlier biographies. I also consider a key visual text which was done with Marley's consent (Morris 2011).

In Verse Three, the primary research content of the book focuses on the radio interviews Marley participated in between 1972 and 1980. These examine the three key contexts in which these interviews took place: Jamaica, Britain, and the USA, which offer distinct ways of hearing things not only contextually, but also in terms of the speaker and the audience. There are also contrasts between mainstream radio and 'specialist reggae DJ formats'. Additionally, it is important to consider Marley in the broader context of how reggae was treated by the mainstream radio in these various contexts through processes of inclusion and exclusion. It is clear from radio data that Marley in many contexts faced processes of exclusion and was not given the same respect or access as many of his popular music contemporaries.

Verse Four focuses on the printed press, in an age when music magazines specifically played a central role in the promotion of popular music. It was without doubt the most time-consuming section to research due to the volume of texts found online. Unlike radio and television in relation to Marley, the printed press, in contexts such as Jamaica, Britain, and the USA, represented him more in terms of volume, coverage, and variety. In order to analyse this more rigorously, I conducted a document analysis of the content, locating several hundred texts and then taking a sample of one hundred for more detailed analysis. The findings produced a number of interesting results on how Marley was represented in these different contexts and again how different types of publication, such as mainstream versus specialist, differed radically. In addition to music publications, the printed press also includes mainstream magazines and newspapers that featured Bob Marley through uniquely luminary narrative examples. I also consider some unique writers who are more notable in the frame of 'gonzo journalism'[3] such as Lester Bangs (2004) and writers who spent time with Marley on the road, such as Vivien Goldman (1979) and Roger Steffens (2018b). It is essential to distinguish between different types of journalists and forms of journalism, as they play a crucial role in defining audiences as distinct groups. Through self-reflection on media content, some journalists even raised question marks on how Marley was misinterpreted. Lester Bangs (2004), Kris Needs (2017), and Neil Spencer (1981) as I will show, did this by touching on issues of language, and how some journalists probably did not understand how Marley spoke in Jamaican 'patwa'[4]. This self-reflection exemplifies a general 'ethnographic turn' in terms of media content and signifies a more critical approach to the practice of journalism itself. Some individuals allowed Marley to speak, while others spoke for and about him in a deliberate manner. I would argue that this applies to all media content of the book, but it is important to note that I came to this conclusion after reading journalistic articles about Bob Marley.

Verse Five considers Bob Marley's limited television appearances as a form of marginal presence, in a similar fashion to his radio appearances, which was a revolution that did not happen. As we shall see, language and marginalisation issues are more prevalent in radio and television. As with radio, there is evidence of Marley's exclusion from mainstream media, especially in Britain and even in Jamaica, where he was rarely featured on television unless he was in the news. Television also employs a variety of interview techniques, from mainstream 'hard talk' (Rinaldo 1978) and distorted documentary news (Negus 1979; Rather 1980) to more community-based and ethnographically-motivated television interviews (Barker 1979; Noble 1980). Also, there is an interesting example of 'gonzo journalism' as television content (Taite 1979). The Verse concludes with television coverage of Marley's death, which is considered significant as a major news story on channels worldwide (Denselow 1981).

Verse Six has a different approach which considers the issue of 'life after death'. Here I argue that the artist we know took on a posthumous and commercially redefined path through the various releases after his death. I also consider the Marley legacy to be uniquely significant in the world of popular music. Clearly he means different things to different people: from a popular music icon to a revolutionary singer to a re-commodified product with an incredible sales record. In many ways these at odds renditions produce a complicated contemporary version of Marley.

Finally, in Verse Seven, which acts as a reprise for the whole book, I summarise the inductive and luminary findings of the research. One of my most important findings relates to how various forms of media influence perceptions of Bob Marley as a popular music icon. In addition, the media contain a wealth of information about Marley, the majority of which I was unaware of prior to beginning this book. Throughout the course of my research, I have discovered a number of surprising and even shocking facts about Bob Marley and the media. Key findings of this book include the ways in which the singer was omitted on purpose and how, even when he was included, he was not always comprehended. I still find it difficult to believe that there was no television interview with Bob Marley produced in Jamaica or Britain. I also emphasise the need for additional research on the musician and the development of a new field of multidisciplinary research called 'Marley Studies'.

NOTES

1. Although the deaths of these popular music artists are completely different, their 'afterlife' as products and commodities have a relative quality. Marley however, as will be shown in Verse Six, leads in terms of posthumous popular music artists after death.

2. Examples of this include: The Official Bob Marley website which includes 'music', 'photos', 'videos' and a 'life and legacy section' (Official Bob Marley 2022); Bob Marley at Discogs featuring 2331 entries (Discogs 2010 'Bob Marley'); Rock's Backpages containing the most comprehensive list of journalistic articles on Marley (Hoskyns 2000); and Midnight Raver featuring a wide variety of media interviews and content with the singer (Midnight Raver 2011).

3. 'Gonzo Journalism' is a subjective form of writing where the author, immersed in a context, becomes a protagonist and writes the story as they have lived or perceived it (Bingley, Hope-Smith, and Rinzler 2012).

4. Patwa or Patois is the oral everyday spoken language of Jamaica.

Verse Two

Too Much Mix Up, Mix Up

There are approximately five hundred books on Bob Marley according to an estimate by Steffens (2018b, Preface). These exist in various languages. As a result, it may appear as if there is a great deal of content to explore. I searched for as much written material as possible but encountered a couple of major impediments. For example, some earlier works are currently out of print and proved difficult to find online. There are also few scholarly works as monographs on the Jamaican singer. This chapter's primary objective is to consider the variety of views on Bob Marley, by bringing together a 'mix up' of biographies and some inspiring academic, visual, and educational works primarily in the form of articles, as well as materials by Marley's immediate relatives. The majority of Bob Marley-related publications were published after his death in 1981 and most are biographical in character. While hundreds of books exist qualitatively, how to categorise them thematically is problematic. A comprehensive annotated bibliography on Bob Marley developing six primary categories is a useful resource thematically. The author's breakdown includes biographies, discographies, photographs, illustrations, songbooks and others (Jurgensen 2009a). At the time the book was released, the author asserted that there were four hundred volumes about Bob Marley, with a heavy emphasis on bibliographies (Jurgensen 2009b, 30).

BIOGRAPHIES ON MARLEY

Generally, as the dominant type of content, biographies on popular musicians often leave many questions unanswered and many pages unturned, particularly given that nobody wrote an official biography, specifically on Bob Marley, while he lived (with his consent). While many ageing musical icons had the luxury of approving the creation of a biography, Marley himself did not have this privilege. An interesting case in the development of this genre of writing in terms of consent and authenticity is *The Beautiful Ones* (Prince and Piepenbring 2019). The book details just as much about Prince as an artist as it does about the process of being a co-author and leaves us wondering if it is a biography, an autobiography, or a co-written biography. Seeing as most of these biographic books on Marley have not reflected on the genre of biography from a critical viewpoint, it is relevant to consider some broader, and more problematic dimensions of this form of writing. What, then, are authors doing when they write a biography?

The first chapter in Hermione Lee's 'Biography: A Very Short Introduction' explains ten guidelines for writing in this occasionally contentious genre. Lee describes biography as reactive: 'You write a biography from the vantage point of where you are: your gender, your race, your class' (Leszkiewicz 2020).

Lee is unromantic about biography as an art form. 'It's not a love affair or a marriage: it's a job' (Wiley and Watt 2019, 187). In doing this 'job', authors should be true, comprehensive, have citations (this is seldom found in most biographies on Bob Marley), be knowledgeable on the subject matter, be objective, and have a respect for history. The subject matter in biographic work is like a 'fish' and the context is the 'stream'. Both, according to Lee, are important. Musical biographies in specific have a tendency to fashion their subjects and investigate how 'myths are created, perpetuated or dispelled' (Wiley and Watt 2019, 187) and these issues are important in understanding how an artist like Bob Marley was represented through this genre. As a pioneer of reggae music and a durable cultural figure, Bob Marley left a lasting effect on contemporary music and as such, after his death, the biographies and other forms of textual representation such as documentaries, aimed to 'tell' and in the process 're-tell' 'his' story. My use of parenthesis in the last sentence is a deliberate political act of questioning the representativeness of who actually speaks through this form of content.

Many of these texts were actually not approved by the artist, which possibly calls into question their validity and depiction. Indeed, a similar argument could also apply to the limited amount of works released during his lifetime. Dalrymple wrote the earliest text I found on Marley in 1976. Although only seventy-seven pages long, I was unable to locate this source first-hand, even though it has also been translated into Greek and German. It has been described as a 'forward-thinking book that has withstood the test of time' and it did not have an International Standard Book Number (ISBN) which makes it even harder to find (Jurgensen 2009b, 32). Another review found online states: 'It was done from the heart and is a beautiful example of an early biography about a revolutionary musician. In addition to the Marley info, the book also includes a few chapters about Rastafari and its history' (Midnight Raver 2012b).

On the other hand, I was able to locate McKnight and Tobler (1977). It was the first publication on Marley with an ISBN number and it is a useful book in terms of detailing the early Wailers, as well as the Trojan and Island years (up to 1977). In my interview with Tobler (2018), the book is explained in the following way:

> What I gave the book company was effectively a cuttings book, using the work of other writers, but the one saving grace was an interview with a man who had worked for the BBC in Jamaica, and knew quite a lot about Marley. The book was published under the title *Bob Marley & The Roots of Regga* by Cathy McKnight & John Tobler by a company known as Star Books. I never heard of it being published anywhere else. (Tobler 2018)

As a result, perhaps the way the book was put together, resembling a kind of jigsaw, makes it fall short of being biographical in an authentic sense. It does contain some valuable insight on the subject of how Rastafarians were viewed at the time in an official police report, reproduced in the *Reading Evening Post* that referred to Rastafarians as a 'West Indian Mafia organization' 'specializing in drugs, prostitution, extortion, protection, subversion and blackmail' (McKnight and Tobler 1977, 138). The report, sourced from Scotland Yard Police, also claimed 'the syndicate's home base is in Jamaica, but they are spreading their operation world-wide. . . . They favour red high powered cars, wear their hair in long rats tails under multicoloured woollen caps, and walk about with their 'prayersticks' – trimmed pick-axed handles' (McKnight and Tobler 1977, 139).

Such depictions provide discursive data on how police authorities perceived and demeaned Rastafarians at that time in Britain. This, as will be shown in subsequent chapters, is radically different from many media depictions of Marley in the British music media.

How much then of the biographic content on Marley is fact or fiction? A good place to start is with one of the first biographies (White 1983).

White's extensive volume (numbering over 600 pages) goes into immense details telling the life of the singer, who started from humble beginnings in Nine Mile, Jamaica. White is often described as a 'giant in music journalism' (Phillips 2002). He focused extensively on Marley, reggae, and Caribbean music and culture for *Crawdaddy*, *Rolling Stone*, *The New York Times,* and he became editor in chief of *Billboard* (Phillips 2002). His biography on Marley was written with approval from Rita Marley, wife and widow to the famous Jamaican artist. It was also based on the fact that the journalist had interviewed and written about Marley for seven years prior to his death, speaking to him on 'two dozen separate occasions' (White 1983, xi). It is the most widely read and revised of all biographies on the singer, which has also been translated into several languages (Jurgensen 2009b, 31).

It was the first Marley biography I read, and I was intrigued by its contextual depth and attention to detail. One review characterises it 'as much ethnography as biography' (Doherty 1984, 370). White's attention to detail, and his constant shifting between objectively re-telling stories and events to subjectively re-framing them leaves the reader thinking to what extent some of the content is accurate biographically or whether it has been reimagined and reconstructed by the author, particularly on issues relating to Marley's 'prophetic' (White 1983, 50–51) 'spirit-like' (White 1983, 91–92) and 'mystical' qualities (White 1983, 183–86), his origins and family (White 1983, 191–92), even down to the intricate re-telling of his birth (White 1983, 49–50). All of this and much more is never credited in terms of sources so it does leave me wondering what is fact and what is fiction. Reading into all this, I came across a relevant interview with Cedella Booker Marley, mother of Bob Marley, where she questions everything about the book:

> Most of what is in it is not facts, I don't know, why or how or where Timothy White got the information(s) that he put in that book. But I am awfully upset with the book and him. Of the things that he talk about us, and these things are not true. . . . I don't see nothing in that book, that Timothy White has written in there that is reality. I know what is reality in there and I know what is foolishness or garbage in other words. (Historic Films Footage Archive 2020)

Around the same time, a second biography emerged (Davis 1983). Stephen Davis is a music journalist based in the USA who has interviewed Bob Marley multiple times. He wrote for *The New York Times, Rolling Stone,* and *The Boston Globe* to name just a few (Davis 2018). He also wrote biographies on Aerosmith and Led Zeppelin (Rasmussen 2017). While his book is considered less fictional and more accurate (Jurgensen 2009b, 31), much of the information contained in it was developed in the same way as White, in other words through previous journalistic interviews and engagements with Marley prior to his death and by interviewing people who knew him. Davis however, makes a really relevant point on language at the start which is important in the context of Marley, language, and media:

> Jamaican English is a language that loses everything when translated to the printed page, and the problem is compounded in a Biography on Bob Marley because of the way he spoke. Bob's words slurred and tumbled into one another in almost total defiance of conventional tense and syntax. And his speech came in different voices, depending on who he was speaking to and how strongly he wanted to make a point. (Davis 1983, ix)

The theme of language and Marley which appears is a recurring theme of my research and this insight by Davis reflects a different type of sensibility as his recordings of Marley were reproduced in the written word, phonetically, as they sounded with the intention 'that Bob tells his own story as much as possible' (Davis 1983, ix). The book has a resourceful bibliography on Marley, featuring many referenced press articles (Davis 1983, 272–93). However, the ending quote, centered in the middle of the page for emphasis, proclaims in a mythologised tone: 'Bob Marley lives, He's a *god*, "History proves"' (Davis 1983, 270). Clearly, this deification and mystification of Marley set the tone for subsequent biographies.

It is not clear, and the same applies to White's biography, if these interviews were conducted with the intention of writing biographically, with the artist's consent to do so, or whether they were a series of journalistic interviews, published previously as various articles, that became biographical content after the singer's death in 1981.

Most of the biographies that followed had the same kind of qualities with one or two exceptions. Of significant note is the biography written by two Jamaican broadcasters (Whitney and Hussey 1984). Again, this is a hard to find, out of print publication, but according to Jurgensen includes interesting press clippings, interview transcripts, and a detailed map of Marley's extensive touring schedule (Jurgensen 2009b, 31). Beyond a plethora of biographic works after the 2000s, a number of more academically inclined books began to emerge. A Professor at South Dakota University wrote two of these in 2007, one of which is biographical (Moskowitz 2007a), while the other focuses on releases and music of Marley (Moskowitz 2007b). The more biographical work by Moskowitz appears without citations and feels like a rehash. It has less sensationalism and is just under 150 pages long (Moskowitz 2007a). The other book feels more interesting in that it charts the singer's development as an artist by releases with reference to context and who he was working with (Moskowitz 2007b). I must say it lacks a methodological approach to analyzing the song content so the title appears to be misleading.

The idea of further biographies on Marley starts to feel a bit pointless by the end of the first decade of the new millennium. However, two new books are exceptions to this rule. They focused specifically on the band groupings Marley was part of or formed. Seasoned British reggae journalist John Masouri explored the complexities of the relationships between the singer and musicians who worked with/for him as The Wailers Band (Masouri 2010). The book gives deep insight into how songs were crafted and describes life on the road as 'The Wailers'. This is interesting as it is the first time musicians around Bob Marley are considered in a substantive way. Masouri also details Aston

'Family Man' Barret's (The Wailers bassist and musical arranger) failed court case against The Marley Estate and Island Records (Masouri 2010).

Another publication looks further back, pre-1972, when the original Wailers included Bob Marley, Bunny Wailer, and Peter Tosh (Grant 2011). The book is as much about The Wailers as it is about the cultural, economic, and political context – Jamaica – that produced the group (Grant 2011). Both of these books contribute to a more critical perspective of the many aspects of how music was made between the artists in these creative collectives as well as the conditions and contexts they lived in.

ACADEMIC WRITING ENTERS THE WORLD OF MARLEY

It is noticeable from 2007 onwards that more academic content starts to emerge and a key publication that laid the groundwork for this was Toynbee's which poses a rather loaded question in its title 'Bob Marley: Herald of a Postcolonial World?' (2007). While this volume is the first detailed academic attempt at grappling with the Marley phenomenon, it is flawed in its hypothetical assumption of a 'third world' artist conquering the 'first world' mainly because, as we shall explain in more depth in Verse Four, Bob Marley completely rejected these definitions,

Despite these concerns, Toynbee was the first writer who engaged an academic framework, namely critical realism, which as he points out required one to 'understand Marley as a social agent and choice-maker, always located within the structure of world capitalism yet by no means completely determined by it' (Toynbee 2007, 11). Since then, surprisingly very little academic monographs exist on Marley, however, a number of scholarly and investigative articles have been published, many of which present interesting and at times contrasting arguments, which I will now turn my attention to.

The posthumous development and exploitation of Marley's works after his death is dealt with in Stephen's interesting contribution to this topic in the context of the USA and how the singer became a mythicised brand reflecting a 'black transnational legacy' (Stephens 1998, 139). From both the view of the 'production of culture' (Peterson 1976) and the 'culture of production' (Negus 1998) Marley becomes more objectified as a commodity after his death. This process is more complicated due to the conflicting demands of the multidimensional character of making songs: authorship, ownership, creativity, legalities, copyright, and essentially who controls what. In Marley's case, after his death, much of this was settled through lengthy, and at times acrimonious, legal cases between the different parties concerned.

An in-depth comprehension of these issues is beyond the remit of this publication, although references will be made to some of these issues in Verse Six. Research and insights on how after signing to Island Records in 1972, the sound of The Wailers changed to appeal more to a white/rock/student radio audience in Britain (Alleyne 2000) are interesting. Alleyne even argues Marley's first Island release 'features a more treble-oriented mix and rhythm tracks accelerated in post-production to attract the rock audience' which raised questions on authenticity (2000, 19). He expands this research to include albums released after the singer's death, including 'Iron Lion Zion' (1992b) and the manner in which the artist's music was altered and decontextualised in later years. The compilation *Legend Remixed* (Marley 2013) features 'one instance the pitch of Marley's vocals were entirely altered to conform to the electronic soundscape' (Alleyne 2019b, 7). This represents mercenary vocal butchery, as altering the actual pitch affects in a relative sense the sound of an artist's voice, their timbre, which is as unique as the human fingerprint. When someone pitch shifts a voice, it is no longer the same voice. This does feel very odd in the context of Bob Marley. Where I disagree slightly with Alleyne is on the more 'treble oriented' sounds of Island's release of *Catch a Fire* (1973a) and the implication that Chris Blackwell changed Marley. Obviously, his career path as an artist took a more international turn post-1972 and he finally, after some fifteen years of largely 'getting burned' in the music industry of Jamaica, started to see a different way of doing things, in terms of production, touring and releasing albums. I can understand the argument that Marley was marketed to a completely different kind of audience; his sound and name from 'The Wailers' to 'Bob Marley and The Wailers' changed but there is something which is troubling with the logic of the commercialization of Marley. This has more to do with the oversimplification of Marley as a thematically and politically complex artist. On every single Island release, Marley unleashes his radicalism, beliefs and philosophies through lyrics and songs in a way that no one had ever done before him. Even on *Kaya* (1978) his tenth studio album, many critics accused Marley of lacking militancy and being lightweight, with reviews such as 'the fire hasn't gone out, but it is on a low flame' (Robins 1978) and 'running on the spot' (Goldman 1977). However, on the same album, song number one side B, 'Time Will Tell' (Marley 1978b) has such a mournful and yet powerful rebellious poetry to it. This is a reflection of Marley's uniqueness as a wordsmith and observer and more than anything, it characterises his multi-vocality because many of his albums have this kind of diversity. My point is that even if Marley was becoming this reframed, commodified global superstar by the early 1970s, his lyrical potency never diminished. In the process of becoming a globalised icon, Marley means many things to many different people and has remained vital in developing a collective sense of imagination that helps us understand the ordering of the world based on inequalities and injustice (Presthold 2020, 175). It is true to say that global presence resonates with much malleability but that the connotations about him have a 'remarkable longevity' (Presthold 2020, 174). So, I cannot accept that Marley's sound had changed after he signed to Island or that his music became more diluted because his beliefs stayed the same and these are reflected through the power of his lyrics as a visionary artist. It is worth considering this further as a counter-argument developed by Gilroy who focuses on what he defines as Marley's 'anti-politics' rooted in humanism.

Gilroy's interesting take on Marley places him in a cultural, historical, and political context that transcends and questions his posthumous commercial exploitation in all manner of products 'from T-shirts, hats, badges, walls and posters' (Gilroy 2005, 226). There is a pervasiveness to his presence as an image, which I even spotted annoyingly in the form of a badly copied image on a beach towel, for sale in a local toy store in Nicosia, Cyprus. While the beach towel made me smile, at the same time it raised questions on just how crass commercialism is. According to Gilroy, Marley's 'utopian politics' (2005, 227), 'cosmopolitan mode' and 'humanistic outlook' (243) provides:

> a new theory and practice of revolutionary agency that accentuate the political will and responsibility of individuals once they have been exposed to truth and stripped of all the illusions that support the injustices of the present in which *we* go hungry while *their* bellies are full. Truth and right are inseparable. Illusions must be burned. (Gilroy 2005, 243)

Key for me in this 'humanist' interpretation of Marley's 'revolutionary agency' as 'anti-politics' (Gilroy 2005, 242) is the way these views flow out of national borders into an 'outernational' realm through a universalism that questions all the wrongs of 'Babylon'–past and present – racism, imperialism, colonialism, capitalism, and all forms of exploitation. The utopian idea that 'another world is possible and Marley serenades its becoming' (Gilroy 2005, 243) has such potency that challenges all the posthumous commercialism and exploitation of sound and image and distils it into a powerful eternal quest for hope and harmony. Gilroy's work stands out in that sense as an astute form of political critique that takes into account diasporic history, culture, and identity.

More recently, to complete the scholarly works, Jacobs (2015) presented a powerful argument locating Marley in the context of Caribbean intellectual 'tradition' alongside 'Hatuey . . . Toussaint Louverture, . . . Blyden,

Henry Sylvester Williams, Marcus Garvey, George Padmore, C.L.R. James, Rex Nettleford, Arthur Lewis, George Beckford, Walter Rodney and Eric Williams' (Jacobs 2015, 1). I find this argument valuable and interesting. Indeed, I would even go one step further by characterizing Marley in the Gramscian tradition of the 'organic intellectual' which in the Caribbean context is also a good description for the revolutionary thinker and writer, Walter Rodney (Hajimichael 2018). Indeed, Jacobs even suggests Marley may have come across Rodney giving public lectures in 1968 at The University of West Indies Mona Campus in Kingston, Jamaica (2015, 5; Rodney 2019).[1]

WORKS BETWEEN ETHNOGRAPHY AND JOURNALISM

I want to now focus on two well-known research publications that fall between academia/ethnography and journalism/fandom. Vivien Goldman is someone who spent a lot of time on the road with Bob Marley in the 1970s. In fact, the writer started out as the singer's first British-based publicist for Island Records and went on the road with him around Britain (McDonnell 2016).

Exodus (Marley 1977a) was recorded while Bob Marley was in exile in London, following the assassination attempt on his life (1976) which Goldman witnessed and retold, along with other key events, such as the Smile Jamaica Concert shortly after (1976) and Marley's exile in London (1976–1978). Goldman's book on the album links scriptures from the Bible to Marley's Rasta liberation messages (Goldman 2006). The book has twelve key chapters, most of which recall the writer's time with Marley over a number of key events, as well as being on the road touring and doing interviews. Verse Eleven 'Exodus A Song Cycle' is broken into ten sub-chapters, detailing each song semiotically and ethnographically with insightful contextual details.

Exodus (Marley 1977a) is an album of two sides that is conceptually and acoustically immaculate. Goldman analyses each song in depth with meticulous detail mixing interview segments with Marley and quotes from the song, which makes a very interesting read. There is also a lot of vital contextualization on Marley's exile in London, and a key point is revealed on his attitude to media, which appears in different ways throughout this publication. This quote is worth considering as it shows a reluctance to be interviewed on his part: 'No publicity hound, Bob was a reluctant interviewee. Once he rather plaintively asked, "Why must it always be me? You can't go and interview Family Man instead? Whenever I speak it always gets me in trouble"' (Goldman 2006, 257).

It is these ethnographic insights that make Goldman's book a vital resource for readers on Marley at this time of his London exile. This reflects, albeit unintentionally on the author's part, hints of 'thick description' (Geertz 1973, 312) which account for human social action by not only including the physical behaviours of the actors, but also their context as perceived by the actors, in order to help us, as outsiders and readers, to understand it better. The demarcation here between a music journalist recalling memories and going through past interviews and a more academically defined ethnographic approach becomes somewhat blurred, which makes Goldman's book an interesting and resourceful read. I would argue this is taken a step further in the next publication (Steffens 2018b).

What is so important about Steffens' work is there are so many ways of seeing and telling things and his attention to detail, with people who knew and worked with Bob Marley, is faultless. Marley in this sense is a complicated human puzzle, which Steffens puts together through a series of stories. The approach is very different from biographic content mentioned earlier in this chapter, which seems to be regurgitating the same stories and themes. Steffens includes more than seventy-five voices and interviews, painting a rich and complex picture of the musician. When used to create a fresh portrayal of a well-known life, oral history can be a powerful technique that adds to data in biographies. Clearly in reading these interviews we get to understand how Marley meant so many different things to so many different people and sometimes the accounts are even contradictory. The book is laden with detailed interviews which give an overall idea that a lot of details on Marley are open to a number of different and often conflicting interpretations. As a result, reading this book leaves us deciding for ourselves on what opinions to form which is a far cry from biographic and often fictionalised accounts. Steffens highlights Marley as a polysemic text as characteristic of Jamaica, an island full of oral interpretations. Quoting an old folk saying, he stresses this point by way of introduction: 'There are no facts in Jamaica, . . . only versions' (Steffens 2018b, epigraph).

IMMEDIATE FAMILY REFLECTIONS

So far, we have looked at works written by people who either knew Marley in a professional capacity or wrote about him from more scholarly perspectives. It is important to also refer to his immediate family members in book form as well, as these works cast a different kind of experiential perspective.[2] I believe this category of work is also important as it offers a perspective that is different from that of biographic work, particularly given the response we noted earlier in this chapter by the singer's mother, Cedella Booker Marley, to White's biography (Historic Films Footage Archive 2020).

Rita Marley's *No Woman No Cry: My Life with Bob Marley* (2005), which was co-written with Hettie Jones, is a different kind of book which came out roughly twenty-five years after the singer died. It gives a specific insight, lacking in other biographies, because it is written from first-hand experience of living with Marley in a familial sense. I believe this makes these texts more grounded. For example, Rita Marley states of Bob Marley's link with reality as a songwriter:

> Georgie did indeed make the fire light, and it was true that it would burn 'through the night'. Bob always wrote about real things, about his feelings. They would be playing guitar and all of us singing and drinking cornmeal porridge or sharing whatever was cooked for the day. All the rest of that song turned out to be true, too. And because Bob was so real, so true to himself, I feel that I need to insist on that here. Aunty always said, 'Don't tell no stories', by which she meant lies. So this is not a 'story', this is my life. (Marley and Jones 2005, 32–33)

Rita Marley uses evocative household imagery on reciprocal nurturing to recall the distant days of mutual affection and just how much things had changed with fame:

> While I was gone Bob would clean the house and cook a meal so we'd have something to eat when we arrived. And there he'd be when the bus pulled up, just as he always said: 'Rita, you look out for me when the bus come, I'll be standing waiting for you'. Years later, when he was called the 'first Third World Superstar' and the 'Negus' of reggae (meaning the 'semi divine Ultimate'), I always wanted to remind people what led there. In St. Ann he had one pair of underpants, which I washed out every night. And if he cared enough to have a meal waiting for me when I came back home from Kingston, I wanted to be back in time to care for him. (Marley and James 2005, 58)

The book by Bob Marley's mother, Cedella Booker Marley, is similar, although it gives a lot more insight into his early years, as a child, as told from a mother's perspective (Marley and Winkler 2015). With this strong sense of knowing where they are coming from, these two works highlight the remarkable journey in a sociological sense from the point of view of changes in social stratification. In one lifetime, Marley leapt from 'country boy' to a worldwide nomadic musical icon.

WORKS WITH AN EDUCATIONAL INTENTION

The next area I want to focus on concerns texts that have a more applied educational purpose. Smith's application of 'transformative education' in 1984 is interesting but feels let down by a sense of shallowness on what he describes as Marley's music. In his own words: 'One striking element of Marley's music is that virtually all of his songs have an upbeat, happy, bouncy feel to them. When listening to his reggae one gets the feeling that God is in heaven and all is right with the world. The phrase, "No problems, mon" comes immediately to mind"' (Smith 1984, 11).

Marley's songs are grouped on two key themes by Smith: 'Rastafarian message and liberation from oppression' (1984, 12) and then a number of songs are explained around these. It is an interesting approach that concludes Marley: 'skillfully blended multiple cultures, syncretistic religious influences, and a commitment to freedom, justice, hope, and unity through the gift of his musical and lyrical genius' (Smith 1984, 11).

I believe the song analysis could have been more substantive and rigorous methodologically in this work. Nevertheless, putting Marley in this transformative education framework is valuable, although the songs are for me very different from a semiotic viewpoint. Another take on this, and a lot more practical, is explained by Wallace, a Jamaican teaching English in France who devised a course on Bob Marley as an 'ideal teaching tool' for students to 'discover Jamaica's history, religion, culture, music, language and politics through a study of his life and works' (Wallace 2009, 1). The paper on this, available online, is a useful resource for anyone wishing to develop course material on Bob Marley for students. Generally, there are a lot more teaching materials available online and The Bob Marley Foundation itself supports numerous educational initiatives in Jamaica, including Bob Marley Primary and Junior High, Chepstowe Basic School, Cedella Booker Basic School, Victory Basic School, Holy Trinity Basic School, Boys Town Basic School, Rhoden Basic School and St. Isaacs Basic School (The Bob Marley Foundation 2022). This for me is an important educational part of Bob Marley's legacy.

VISUAL REPRESENTATIONS

Finally, I want to refer to the visual and illustrative works. I will not discuss these in detail, however, because they are at times repetitious (sometimes employing the same photographs over time) and contain elements of self-promotion (something which is common in several biographical works as well). However, a mention is pertinent to one inspiring photographic work

(Morris 2011). At the age of seventeen, Dennis Morris accompanied Bob Marley on tour as a photographer and ended up becoming a close friend, snapping photographs of Marley which ended up on covers of *Time Out* and *Melody Maker* (Morris 2022). His images of the singer have a special intimacy and candidness. More than anything, this book reveals a relationship between the photographer and subject being photographed as an act of mutual respect and authenticity (Morris 2011). I find this work to be more authentic than reading many biographies, most of which were not sanctioned or approved by the singer himself. Morris' images articulate an element of consent that many other biographic works lack.

By way of conclusion, this concept is essential for comprehending how Marley has been portrayed, frequently without his presence or agreement. It is also essential to comprehend this notion of the 'version' in terms of oral history/reflections on the artist and the artist's polysemic character. As a global cultural figure, he represents different things to many individuals. This is also clear through his close associates and their own recollections (Steffens 2018b). The artist is also a powerful force of alternative political thinking (Gilroy 2005). In trying to unravel his works, we not only get to understand the context of the time and the meaning of the songs (Goldman 2006), but we also get a sense of what the songs mean to us, and how we negotiate their meaning into our own contexts, which makes Marley a malleable cultural icon and political figure (Presthold 2020, 176). At the same time however, the commercialization of remixes after he passed away is problematic in terms of authenticity and the integrity of Marley's works (Alleyne 2019b).

Taking all of this into account, understanding existing literature on Marley is not as straightforward as it might appear. He is an enigmatic and unique popular icon. Do these commercialised consuming masses comprehend the intricacies of his Rasta worldview, despite their familiarity with his songs popularised on the *Legend* (Marley 1984) compilation? As a popular figure, Marley is all of these and more at the same time. He is an example of the sociological term intersectionality (Crenshaw 2012) where so many factors need to be understood in terms of his experiences and vocal resistance through songs to different forms of oppression. Marley is not a singular entity; his multi-vocality, visionary songs, and polysemy raise challenges about how he has been portrayed and how different works have reflected upon him.

A revolutionary, an artist who progressed from a village in Jamaica to be known throughout the world, a product reframed time and time again to reap more profits for multinational music companies which often leads to the equation 'Reggae = Bob Marley'. Marley in this sense then is like an open book, as he has a unique malleability which can be interpreted in so many different ways. Hsu reflects on this almost as if the artist did it deliberately: 'His lyrics lent themselves to a kind of universalist reading of exodus and liberation. He was one of the first pop stars who could be converted into a life style. Bob left that open, too' (2017).

As an afterthought on this flexibility of Marley in terms of collective memory, and even a sense of memorialization (Hajimichael 2010), it is pertinent to refer to a classic contemporary novel (James 2015). Although James does not mention Marley by name–he always refers to Marley as 'the singer' – the book is a lucid fictionalised interpretation of the assassination attempt on Marley's life in December 1976. It reads like an endless stream of detailed versions, with ever-changing perspectives, overlapping, contradicting, appearing completely unique, and giving a kaleidoscopic rendition of Jamaican life at the height of political sectarianism. Although it is fiction, reading attentively, I cannot help but think just how close or far from the truth James' account actually is. However, in that version, in a way that is very characteristic of Jamaica (Steffens 2018b preface), James tells a complete story through a series of interconnected and often, contradicting ones. Even if Marley is not mentioned by name, the link is clear, and the universality of his message, shines as always through his work: 'But in another city, another valley, another ghetto, another slum, another favela, another township, another intifada, another war, another birth, somebody is singing Redemption Song, as if the Singer wrote it for no other reason but for this sufferah to sing, shout, whisper, weep, bawl, and scream right here, right now' (James 2015, 601).

That universalism and sense of humanity drew me to Marley's music, since his inclusiveness reflected my own experiences of injustice and inequality. Much later, I was curious about how he had been portrayed in the media, which is the subject of the remainder of this book.

NOTES

1. An important part of Walter Rodney's book *The Groundings with My Brothers* (2019) was developed through reasoning/conversations with Rastas in the ghettos of Kingston, Jamaica. It may even be likely that he knew of Marley or met him during his stay in Jamaica.

2. There are a number of other books written by family members including 'Bob Marley, My Son' (2003) by Cedella Booker Marley; and various books referencing the meaning and significance of songs and the language of Marley by Cedella Marley, Bob and Rita Marley's oldest daughter. Such books include 'Every Little Thing: Based on the song "Three Little Birds" by Bob Marley' (2015) and 'Get Up, Stand Up' (2019). These are aimed at young children for educational purposes.

Verse Three

Radio Waves Limiting the Gong

This chapter looks specifically at radio interviews and Marley in particular historical contexts, namely Jamaica, Britain, and the USA. These three countries represent the vast majority of radio interviews featuring the artist.[1] My intention is to explore what these media engagements tell us about Marley in terms of media representation, in other words what radio, as a medium, reflected about the artist in these radically different contexts. I must confess a point of caution here with regard to 'representation' and 'meaning' and radio interviews, being interpreted post-text. They operate not as isolated incidents, but as something more complex and constitutive of how we might interpret a particular singer (Hall 1997, 8). What radio 'said' about Marley as a medium cannot and should not be characterised in a one-dimensional manner. By exploring radio interview data, through listening and re-listening, I have come up with a set of conclusions grounded in the data subject matter and linked to a variety of historical contexts. In other words, what radio said about Marley was dependent on context, and who conducted the interviews, in terms of what type of radio media. Before elaborating further on my key findings, an explanation on methodology is required as well as some introductory thoughts on the link generally between popular music and radio as a medium.

DATA COLLECTION AND METHODOLOGICAL ISSUES

I found a wealth of information that raised a number of methodological concerns from the outset. The validity and authenticity of data collected online is problematic. While it is easy to collect data online, imagine for instance trying to locate interviews with any artist, in their physical recorded form, from different sources around the world. The internet provides us with a vast online archive, which is useful for researchers. However, some of the issues found with media data collected online include mistaken, discredited, or disputed information. At times, this caused some confusion over when and where interviews took place or even whether they took place at all. One way of ameliorating this is triangulation and avoiding relying on just one source of online information. Seeking different online sources proved to be a useful method for getting a better and more reliable picture. Two different websites provided data for tracing media content on Bob Marley.[2] These sites are fan sites or administered by people with a deep knowledge of Marley. In order to study the content from these different websites, the following method was adopted: data were firstly categorised by date, followed by location, town, country, and then by type of media engagement.

Issues of representation are central to the research. A noticeable question that arises in any research reliant on online data as its main source of information is its comprehensiveness. We cannot argue, for example, that the interviews under study are the only interviews Marley did; more may exist but they were not found online from the sources examined. Therefore, while it is impossible to say my data are complete, the analysis has relied only on evidence that exists.

Additionally, every attempt was made to relate data to different situations and their respective audiences. There is a need for digital/online research to emphasise this trait even more because media studies research is typically interdisciplinary (Corner 1998; Kellner 2003; Livingstone 2005; Sholle 1995; Streeter 1995). Radio interviews are more than just audio snapshots of contexts that can be accessed online for nostalgic purposes; they also represent specific relationships between the interviewer and the subject of the interview and are a part of something much larger in terms of how particular artists are portrayed.

Lastly, it is important to acknowledge that this research only considers analysis of radio interviews. This is by no means representative of radio in a comprehensive sense which would include other significant variables such as song airplay, representation of genres, inclusion in news features and conversational references by presenters. Attempting to analyze all of this across many countries however is a huge task well beyond my reach.

POPULAR MUSIC AND RADIO AS A MEDIUM

Radio reaches anyone who listens to it and from early in on its development it was considered a sign of 'modernity' and 'the world's greatest advancement' in terms of electronic media in the twentieth century (Taylor 2002, 426).

Radio and popular music have 'influenced' each other in 'intricate' ways that are interdependent (Michelsen and Krogh 2016, 2). Radio needs music and the music industry needs radio for its content to be heard and this was a prevalent relationship in the development of popular music:

> In the period 1920–50 the radio and music industries developed a symbiotic relationship. Music on record became the basis of radio programming; radio play became the basis of record selling. Radio was crucial for the emergence of new popular music genres (jazz and blues and swing and hillbilly), and just as important for the making and marketing of classical records. (Frith 2002, 226)

Referring to the world and Belgian context in specific, Di Spurio notes: 'from 1949 to 1960, the number of radio sets owned increased from 150 million to 370 million worldwide' (2017, 547). Moreover, radio and music were essential aspects of 'youth culture' which 'became a distinct social group with its own rites, codes, and practices, as well as its own radio shows' (Di Spurio 2017, 547).

Additionally, it is worth considering the role of the radio DJ in these processes, often as a kind of expert and taste-maker, which by the 1970s led to many radio DJs also becoming frequent writers and TV personalities. John Peel, for example, would also write for magazines such as *Let It Rock* (1974), *Disc & Music Echo* (1968–73), *International Times* (1969), and *Sounds* (1973) (Peel 2010). Peel presented *Top of the Pops,* the leading TV chart show, from the 1960s until the 1990s (John Peel Wiki 2022b). This convergence between disc jockey/taste-maker/writer would become a key thing in the development of a format, which perhaps has been largely ignored historically, namely the 'interview' with a popular music artist. On radio this was inevitably someone who was knowledgeable on the subject matter, otherwise the interview would have sounded baseless, irrelevant and badly researched. The insight and connectedness of radio DJs to interview people on air would lead to significant ethnographic inroads into the lives of musicians and their narratives. A good example of this phenomenon is considered at length in this chapter with reference to one of the only in-depth interviews with Bob Marley in Britain (Rodigan 1980).[3]

BOB MARLEY AND RADIO—KEY FINDINGS

With hindsight, having collected data through various online sources, I conclude that Bob Marley's interview presence on radio was somewhat limited. There are also issues with missing content. At least five of the seventeen radio interviews (two in the USA and three in the UK) referenced are not readily available to be heard. One of these was with Paul Gambaccini on BBC Radio 1 (British Broadcasting Corporation). When I interviewed the renowned radio presenter for this research, he told me his Marley interview happened live on air in 1975 (Gambaccini 2018) but there was no archive of it.

A clear finding of the data is that all the interviews happened on English-speaking radio broadcasting outlets. This is predictable, given that radio as a medium cannot have subtitles, and overdubbing a voice in translation would have been more time-consuming, costly, patronizing to the artist and annoying to audiences listening. Additionally, the interviews enabled me to distinguish between different types of categories grounded in the data findings. These are broadly divided between mainstream, fan-based/reggae specialists, and Black media/community outlets. These categories are by no means exclusive as there was some overlap, although clearly there was no representation that reflected mainstream/Black media. Furthermore, a key finding of this chapter is the more knowledge someone had of Marley and his music, the more enriched the interview was. Obviously, as we shall hear, this means mainstream radio tended to approach Marley along lines of superficial questioning. I want to take this issue further to the level of language and comprehension, in other words, how people in media in general reacted to how the artist spoke. For instance, Benjamin Foot, the first tour manager of The Wailers 'confessed that he often found it impossible to decipher what was being said by The Wailers in the early 1970s' (Grant 2011, 145). As we will see, language miscomprehension happened a lot in the 1970s on radio with Marley outside Jamaica.

I would like to turn first to findings about the content of the interviews in Jamaica – where it all began.

RADIO IN YARD – MARLEY'S JAMAICA RADIO INTERVIEWS

Marley's development as an artist has three stages. Firstly, 1962–1973 – the formation and development of The Wailers, a largely local phenomenon; secondly, 1973–1980 – the main international globalization of his works; and finally, 1981–present – life after death. It is very difficult to analyze the early period, defined as 'murky' largely due to a lack of documentation on record sales and chart positions (Unterberger 2017, 20). Having read many biographies on Marley, this period is clearly one of struggle and hardship. The two existing radio stations, JBC (Jamaican Broadcasting Company) and RJR (Radio Jamaica and Rediffusion) had control over song airplay, with close links to established music producers and distribution companies. Alan 'Skill'

Cole, a well-known footballer, friend and road manager of Bob Marley during this time describes these media oligopolies in depth (Steffens 2018b, 112).

Marley, then, like many Jamaican artists during this period, found it difficult to get airplay and proper income from his music. There is even an argument that Marley was seldom played on radio in Jamaica during this time (Cuthbert and Brown 1997, 144), which I will return to later. Going one step further, the subject of radio in general in Jamaica with regard to reggae, and local music forms is significant contextually. Surprisingly the first 24-hour reggae station was established in 1990. Irie FM broke the mold (Chat-Bout 2022). It feels strange, if not surreal, that some thirty years after reggae emerged from Jamaica, a radio station finally opened playing just reggae on the island.

More recently, Rose, the general manager of the Jamaica Association of Composers, Authors and Publishers Limited (JACAP) noted: 'Too much foreign music is played, and hence, we have to remit quite a lot of our distribution to foreign societies. In 2015, 82 percent of the royalties went overseas, in 2013, 85 percent went overseas, and in former years such as 2006, 63 percent went overseas' (Rose 2016).

These glaring omissions are even more evident when considering the historical exclusion of Rastas by mainstream Jamaican media.[4] For example, Vere Johns is described as 'the most influential man in Jamaican music in the second half of the 1950s' (Bradley 2001, 19). His *Opportunity Knocks Talent Show* on RJR provided many local artists with their first breaks as singers. Grant recalls a story about dancer Margareta Mahfood and Count Ossie and the Rasta Drummers who accompanied her on Johns Christmas Show in 1956 where the presenter insisted the Rastas could not be on the stage. Mahfood stood her ground, even saying she would not dance without them. Johns included them but ensured they were at the back of the stage, dimly lit, and barely visible (Grant 2011, 55). Symbolically, this act of inclusion/exclusion indicates how media in Jamaica perceived Rasta culture discursively and politically. It is also important to recognise how Bob Marley, after becoming a Rastafarian, had a completely different experience of life in Jamaica. Rastas were excluded on many levels, and this is something he would experience for himself first hand. For example, he experienced this at his first meeting with Danny Sims,[5] the African American music producer who was partners with Johnny Nash in the label JAD. The initials for the label being based on the first names of its three founders, Johnny Nash, Arthur Jenkins and Danny Sims (Kenner 2012). On his way to the meeting in Russell Heights by bicycle, the police stopped Marley and told him to turn back to the ghetto. On arrival at the meeting, the servants in Sims house refused to serve Marley due to his dreadlocks (Grant 2011, 151).

Change, in this sense, in terms of representations of Rasta in the medium of radio was a long time coming. Something happened though in the late 1970s through the radio phenomenon of Mikey Dread. As one of the key pioneers in reggae on radio, Mikey Dread started a four-hour show on JBC entitled *Dread at the Controls*, during the late-night Saturday shift in 1976. Mikey Dread set the tone for generations of reggae DJs that followed him, leading to it becoming the number one radio show in Jamaica in 1977 (Clayson 2008).

Bizarrely this was one of the few Jamaican radio shows to feature roots reggae, as the rest were obsessed with U.S. soul, country and western, and pop of any quality. His show featured tailor-made jingles in Jamaican patois by himself and well-known artists. These were featured because the management at JBC insisted he should not speak, so the music spoke for itself with the jingles. Mikey Dread's authenticity both put him at odds with his establishment employers and thus created the first Jamaican Roots reggae radio legend. At the same time though, this appearance of a Rasta on radio signifies a partial acceptance of just one DJ. Initially marginalised, late on a Saturday night, but still on mainstream radio in Jamaica, cassette tapes of Mikey Dread's shows would soon go around the world as bootlegs and pave the way for a whole new generation of Reggae radio presenters who emerged after him, such as David Rodigan, Tony Williams, and The Dread Broadcasting Corporation, DBC. Mikey Dread represented a revolution in Reggae on the radio. As he describes it: 'With *Dread at the Controls* it was just me, and apart from the jingles, everything is live. *Live, live, live* . . . It was taking sound-system technique to the radio, and programming the radio to fit the Jamaican society – *not the other way round*' (Bradley 2001, 477).

With this kind of background in mind, three key people interviewed Bob Marley in Jamaica: Neville Willoughby, Dermot Hussey, and Ron Sinclair.

Willoughby was a well-known radio presenter, journalist, and singer, who worked on both RJR and JBC. His first interview with Marley was in 1973, recorded on location in Bull Bay, Jamaica. It is characteristic that from the outset, Willoughby refers to Marley as 'Bob' in the first person, a clear indication of the interview being relaxed, informal and the interviewer being comfortable with Marley and vice-versa (Willoughby 1980).

The interview sounds more like a conversation between two friends, with Willoughby building a number of themes on how Marley started, 'if he is a bitter person' (thematically in his songs) and whether it is different playing in Jamaica and playing abroad. Often between questions or as Marley speaks, Willoughby can be heard conversing/reacting in a colloquial and conversational tone to some of this answers. I would even argue this interview (like Goldman and Steffens in the previous Verse) has an ethnographic quality reminiscent of 'thick description' (Geertz 1973, 312). The following extract gives an idea of this tone:

Neville Willoughby: Yeah, yeah, yeah.

Bob Marley: So it's not angry and all of that but it's just truth and it has to burst out of a man like a river.

Neville Willoughby: Right, right. And your way to burst it out is in your music? That's the way it comes out. That's your expression?

Bob Marley: Well, well, yes. That's how we talk.

Neville Willoughby: Alright, listen now. You talk about material things, right? But Bob quite frankly I don't think you would fairly say that right now you are a sufferer in the sense of money.

Bob Marley: Well, if you check what money is then money doesn't make you suffer and money doesn't make you not suffer. Hey, everything really rest in your mind. Because dig this. I am a farmer, you know and I do live with money. They could never give me a penny and I have to live. But again I can play music and I am not afraid of the earth. So I play music and if money should come out of music let money come out of music; it is not that my heart is really opened wide and bleeding blood to get money.

Neville Willoughby: Yeah, right. (Willoughby 1980)

A second interview conducted by Willoughby happened in Jamaica in 1978. Both these interviews were later released by Neville Willoughby as 'The Bob Marley Interviews' with side A of the vinyl being conducted in 1973 and side B in 1978 (Willoughby 1980). Another five releases (with the same content) have come out on various labels (Discogs 2022a). There is also evidence online that Marley himself objected to the release and commercialization of these interviews, according to a comment by Dakodisc on the Discogs web page: 'According to THE BEAT magazine volume 21 number 3 released in 2002: Bob Marley caused production to be suspended on Neville Willoughby's first attempt at releasing recordings of his landmark interviews from 1973 and 1978' (Dakodisc 2015).

These interviews do remain, however, as possibly the most informed category of Marley interviews done from Jamaica (and worldwide) by someone who knew Marley from as far back as 1968, which gives us a clear idea of how at ease Willoughby was in his company. In that year Marley took a break from music with Peter Tosh, Bunny Wailer, and Rita Marley, returning to farming in Nine Mile, his birth place, in the parish of St. Ann, Jamaica. At the time Willoughby was producing his first television talk show called *See't Yah* (Steffens 2018b, 92) which featured a short program filmed in Marley's home parish. It is described by broadcaster as 'The Legendary Film of Bob Marley on the Donkey' and sadly this first ever appearance of Marley on television in Jamaica was not saved anywhere in archival form (Steffens 2018b, 93).

Another acclaimed Jamaican broadcaster, Dermot Hussey, carried out an informed and significant interview. The date for this interview is often cited as 1975 online but as the broadcaster says himself, it was conducted in 1974, and this was a significant year in that it was when the original Wailers–Bob Marley, Bunny Wailer, and Peter Tosh, disbanded as a band. Here it is worth considering some background anecdotal evidence reflected by Hussey:

> At the time of the breakup of the Wailers, I had approached Bob about doing an interview. As I lived near to 56 Hope Road and in fact passed the house everyday going to work at JBC, I would wait until after he played soccer, as a ritual every afternoon and I kept asking him to do the interview. I think a week passed. Nothing. Then another week, and then unknown to me Skill Cole convinced him that he should do the interview. Bob had one stipulation. He didn't want to do it at the JBC, so find somewhere else. I did. A studio off Hope Road that did jingles and commercials. With all the excitement, I never remembered to note the day in 1974 that it took place. But he arrived promptly, and in the course of the interview he was very outspoken. He was clearly upset by feedback that he was getting about what Tosh was saying about it, the break up. In fact, after the interview, sometime after it was broadcast, he told me to destroy it. 'You see that interview? It could value a million dollars, as well as it could value nothin'. I gave him a copy of the tape but against his wishes I never destroyed the tape. (Midnight Raver 2014a)

The same story is also evident elsewhere (Steffens 2018b, 182) and in a similar light as Willoughby, this interview is conversational and relaxed, and conducted by someone who was familiar with Marley's work and progress. Furthermore, like Willoughby, this interview was commercially released as *Talkin' Blues* (Marley 1991) with songs being interspersed between edit cuts of the interview (Marley 1991). It is interesting to note as well that Marley did not want to do the interview at JBC; this is further evidence of his aversion towards Jamaican Radio Stations as institutions. Additionally, both Willoughby and Hussey commercialised their interviews. Marley clearly was not happy with this, due to the content particularly in Hussey's interview, and points on the break-up of The Wailers (Steffens 2018b, 182), but inevitably they were not the last people to try to monetise radio interview content featuring Bob Marley.

Finally, regarding Jamaican radio content, Ron Sinclair conducted a brief phone interview in 1980 on JBC Radio. This regarded rumours that had circulated about Marley being dead (Sinclair 1980). Referring again to Marley in the first person as 'Bob', the interviewer covers various topics in just over two minutes, such as Marley having cancer (which the artist dismisses), politics, the One Love Peace Concert 1975, and Marley being shot. Sinclair is totally upfront with his line of questioning:

> *Sinclair:* . . . a lot of things have been said all week long Bob in Jamaica and of all the things people say you're dead.
>
> *Marley:* Mi Dead? . . . A lot of people haffe dead leave me, you know, Ha!!! *(translates as 'Me, dead? A lot of people have died left me, you know, Ha!!)'* (Sinclair 1980)

In this interview, Marley's voice sounds different. I am not sure if it was due to his illness, as he sounds angered by the assumptions around his alleged death. In the entire interview collection, which I have heard from around the world in different formats, and despite some often rather naive and misinformed lines of questioning, Marley never sounded angry. His voice has a different pitch, which with hindsight, makes me doubt the authenticity of this interview.

The way that radio represented Marley in Jamaica was entirely different. In general, he was 'Bob' – always referred to by his first name – and the interviews he gave to Neville Willoughby and Dermott Hussey have a different quality. At the same time, these Jamaican radio moments with Marley appear sparse, even limited considering his eventual fame around the world. Mikey Dread sums up radio in Jamaica as a misrepresentative medium: 'They tried to ruin our culture by imposing on us a foreign culture and foreign programming. The man just don't want to play certain music, they think reggae is for lower class – *they don't even play Bob Marley.* Them is Jamaican people who act like they are not black' (Bradley 2001, 475).

Although we are not addressing the issue of airplay in-depth, in an interesting anonymous interview by a Jamaican that Eric Clapton's 'I Shot the Sheriff' sold more copies than Marley's (the original writer) in Jamaica it is claimed 'The test was on airplay, and Clapton won hands down' (McKnight and Tobler 1977, 128). I find that hard to believe but there is one possible explanation – that Marley was played much more in Jamaica after he died. As Clyde McKenzie[6] noted on the day of Marley's death in May 1981:

> I was with my friends next door. It was at a spot where we hung out and I learned a lot about Jamaican music. I recall hearing this deluge of his music being played on Jamaican radio . . . it was endless Marley. I was hearing music that I never knew existed, and had never been played on radio like this. (Johnson 2020)

BRITAIN – RADIO – FROM ATTEMPTS AT ASSIMILATION TO DAVID RODIGAN

Britain is a strategic place in the development of reggae as a music genre due to migration from the Caribbean which is known as 'The Windrush Generation', made up of people who came over initially on the ship *The Emperor Windrush* in 1948. The cultural and political influences of this population movement span some six generations to the formation and hybridization of many music genres and styles such as MC/Soundsystems, UK ska/2-tone, jungle, drum 'n' bass, 2-step/UK garage, grime, and of course, reggae. However, all of that did not happen in a harmonious manner, as being different, and being heard in an often hostile society, was by no means easy:

> The Windrush generation and their descendants faced unprecedented levels of racialised exclusion, racial violence and institutional racism. Yet they built lives, families, neighbourhoods and cultural institutions – like the sound systems – that transformed the cultural life of Britain's cities and put potent strains of afro-diasporic art and culture into circulation, for the benefit of all. (Melville 2020)

We can trace the relationship between Britain and reggae back to mainstream radio's reception of the music in the 1960s. There is no entity more institutional in radio than the British Broadcasting Corporation (BBC). From the late 1960s, when reggae morphed from ska in Jamaica, the BBC marginalised the music: 'It was shunned by British radio. Radio 1's number-one DJ, Tony Blackburn, dismissed it as "rubbish". Record labels even started doing remixes, reducing the bass and adding an orchestral feel to sweeten the music, making it more palatable to the British ear, in a bid to get it onto the UK airwaves' (Marre 2011).

This practice was called 'stringsing up', and it led to a number of remixed reggae songs being played on mainstream radio, such as 'Help Me Make It Through the Night' by John Holt, as well as 'Young Gifted and Black' by Bob and Marcia (Riley 2014, 107). The watering down of reggae, giving it that 'poppy sensibility' (Finlaysan 2010) and making it more digestible to 'white', 'mainstream', 'pop' audiences (highly contentious terms, hence the quotation marks), was also evident in a number of novelty-based white acts – the 'black and white minstrels of reggae' – who exploited the music. Producer Jonathan King's 1971 'Johnny Reggae' by the one-hit-wonder group The Piglets (who were in fact actors narrating over a backing track) may have entered the pop charts, but it was never played on the sound systems that were 'the main media for the music' in the late 1960s and early 1970s (Bradley 2001, 79). Additionally, it was 'lamentable' and 'audibly jarring' but played by BBC Radio, which at the time avoided reggae by Black and Jamaican artists (Bradley 2001, 256).

The first radio appearance that Marley did in Britain was in 1973, when the original Wailers line-up played live on the BBC Radio 1 program *Top Gear* in a live studio session presented by John Peel.[7] This was also The Wailers' first ever live appearance in Britain. The band appeared twice in the same year on *Top Gear* (John Peel Wiki 2022a). In the second show, Bob Marley is featured in his first radio interview, with John Peel, who, given the limited data that exists online, spent his time confirming Marley's statement with 'uh-hum' between the singer's words. I was unable to find the complete interview but a short snippet exists online (*Top Gear* 1973). Peel, a radio legend in his own unique way, went from the pirate radio station Radio Caroline to BBC Radio 1, and was viewed as a progressive voice who always championed reggae music (John Peel Wiki 2022a). He provided interesting insights on the BBC's reluctance to play reggae in the late 1960s and on Bob Marley and The Wailers auditioning at the BBC through a unique anecdote:

> Bob Marley and the Wailers failed their BBC audition because in the view of the panel they didn't know how to play reggae! Which, was, er, you get some kind of, er, the BBC dance orchestra doing a strict tempo version of reggae, and people would say 'ah, that's how Reggae should be'. (Gordon and Connolly 2002)

It is not clear whether this audition actually took place or whether Peel was talking allegorically against the background of 'stringsed-up' reggae songs being the acceptable sound of the genre for the BBC. Whatever the case, clearly, in its authentic form reggae was marginalised by the BBC. The first full interview featuring Bob Marley was by Paul Gambaccini, who told me: 'I well recall my interview with Bob Marley, which took place in the Island Records offices in St. Peters Square in Hammersmith, West London, in (I believe) 1975. A twenty-minute piece was broadcast on BBC Radio 1, and I wrote an article that appeared in *Esquire* magazine' (Gambaccini 2018).

Gambaccini was not a reggae specialist. At the time, he worked on BBC Radio 1 as a mainstream music reporter who started out at the BBC in 1973 as a reporter on John Peel's program *Rockspeak* (Gambaccini 2018). Unfortunately, it was not possible to locate Gambaccini's interview online or in his own radio archive.

The next radio interview happened in 1980, and it is the only in-depth interview readily available online in its original form. This was with David Rodigan on Capital Radio, a commercial radio station based in London (Rodigan 1980). Note the time gap. For five years Bob Marley was completely absent from radio in Britain as far as interviews go, although his songs were played often on air. Again this shows his limited presence on the medium of radio. The year 1980 also saw Marley interviewed with Aston 'Family Man' Barrett (bass player in The Wailers) on a radio station in London; and a Marley interview on radio in Manchester. Despite online references to these radio interviews, recordings of the full shows with full production credits could not be found.

The interview by David Rodigan has a historical significance as it is the only lengthy, archived British on-air interview with Bob Marley that we have access to and as such is worthy of in-depth analysis. The interview was the first of its kind in that Rodigan was a reggae enthusiast from his teens. He was a connoisseur of the genre and one of only two people on commercial radio (the other being the late Tony Williams on Radio London) to have a specialist reggae radio show. This kind of interview leads us to a unique category of people who interviewed Marley on radio who were deeply engrossed in his music as fans and collectors.

As such, Rodigan's interview was in-depth and well-informed, following a chronological order and reflecting on Marley's development up to his new material and on the evolution and break-up of the original Wailers (and whether they would ever reunite). Nowhere during the interview was there any evidence of disconnection or any kind of misunderstanding, which is largely due to Rodigan's awareness of Bob Marley's songs as a catalogue of significant cultural work.

In many ways, Rodigan's interview reflects a common trend that followed in many other interviews (such as those that we will explore in the next section on the USA) as a case of a kind of on-air, well-informed fandom. Rodigan worshiped the early works of The Wailers and in his biography states: 'In Bob's lyrics – whether they are about love, broken hearts or social injustice – he had something to say for everyone. When people discover his work they become fans for life' (Rodigan 2017, 1).

Another intriguing fact about the Rodigan interview, again relating to his enthusiasm, is the sound or pitch of his voice. He discusses this quite lucidly in his biography:

> I was so nervous that in the interview you can hear my voice is higher than it normally would be. My heart was beating so fast it was affecting my breathing. I was actually shaking because I was in the presence of Bob Marley and I was going to do a live interview with him. (Rodigan 2017, 8)

Finally, the interview also featured an exclusive piece of music – 'Could You Be Loved' (Marley 1980) – that was brought to the studio at Capital Radio by Bob Marley on an original master tape. This was the first time that song was played on air. The interview ends with the song, and Rodigan and Marley have an informal conversation between friends: 'Good luck with the new single, good luck with the new album when it comes out and thanks very much for coming on the show. Bob used one word to respond: "Nice"' (Rodigan 2017, 11).

Despite the positivity of the Rodigan interview, there is also evidence suggesting Marley's exclusion by the mainstream, represented largely by the BBC. Rock critic John Tobler interviewed Marley three times in the 1970s. These interviews, scheduled through Island Records, had the aim of getting Bob Marley featured on the BBC Radio (Tobler 2018). Despite the quality of the interviews, as Tobler states: 'Bob was not used on Radio 1 because it was felt that his Jamaican patois would not be comprehensible to many listeners' (Tobler 2018).

It is hard to believe this kind of marginalization and partiality, considering Marley's eventual popularity. To conclude, despite the enthusiasm and well-informed interview with David Rodigan, Bob Marley was marginalised by mainstream British radio in interviews. Obviously, his songs got played on radio and featured on television, but as a popular celebrity he only appeared in interview form on radio in Britain four times in the last seven years of his life, which reflects a form of underrepresentation. This is even more striking since Marley had become a globalised music commodity by the end of the decade under examination. His sole appearance in Italy, for instance, at the San Siro Stadium on 27 June 1980, attracted one hundred thousand people, a record at time for a music concert (Pino and Venditti 2021). In May of the same year, Marley played for Zimbabwe's independence celebrations in Harare. I mention all this to reflect on where Marley played his last ever gig in Britain, at Staffordshire New Bingley Hall – not quite San Siro (Concert Archives 2022). Marley, being interviewed on Capital Radio, had a limited appeal as Rodigan's Roots Rockers had a 'specialist' identity and airtime at 10 p.m. until midnight on Saturday. This is meager compared to media exposure of pop stars of that era. David Bowie, for example, guested as a DJ on BBC Radio 1 on 20 May 1979, selecting music for two hours (Open Culture 2015). When members of Queen did radio interviews, they were often with mainstream DJs such as Kenny Everett on Capital Radio (Everett 1976), and with DJ John Brown on BBC Radio over two episodes (Brown 1977). Marley never had the equivalent qualitative presence on 'mainstream' radio despite his worldwide fame and popularity by the late 1970s. The closest he came to the mainstream on British radio was live appearances on John Peel and an interview with Paul Gambaccini.

There is a saying on radio and in the music business that forms part of what people call 'common sense' in marketing and promotion. I cannot really attribute this to any academic source, but it is a saying I have heard many times: 'To get the airplay you always need the hits, but to get the hits you need the airplay'. It is a tautological situation. Marley clearly had the hits during the 1970s, but he was not given that airtime on radio in Britain in a narrative sense as a featured guest. The formula in the USA was slightly different. By the end of the decade, Marley was determined to crack the mainstream.

RADIO IN THE USA – THE LAST FRONTIER

As in Britain, radio interview exposure of Marley in the USA was limited in a mainstream sense. Like the Tobler interviews that were not aired by the mainstream in Britain, a similar instance was found in a candid *Vanity Fair* article in which Jo Maeder recalls an interview with Marley that she did for Y-100 Radio (a mainstream station) in South Florida in 1980.[8] However, in all the online data explored, there is no listing of this interview or its content, because it never aired on radio. A higher decision maker at the station asked Maeder: 'Ever hear him [Marley] on Y-100?' (Maeder 2016).[9] Frank Crocker[10] endorses this kind of institutional practice in commentary to Danny Sims about potential airplay of Marley's songs in the USA: 'Danny, you bring your gun, your dope, your money but this material here, you gotta bring a translator. It'll never be played on the R & B stations' (Grant 2011, 174).

With this introductory background in mind, existing data for the USA suggest eight appearances by Marley on radio, an estimated two of which, by Roger Steffens, were actual backstage recordings that were later edited and used on air (Steffens 2018a). A large number of American radio DJs were in many ways, like Rodigan in Britain, reggae and Marley enthusiasts. Roger Steffens, one of the founders of *The Beat* magazine, produced and presented *Reggae Beat* on radio station KCRW-Los Angeles (College Radio Workshop) from 1979 to 1987 (Steffens 2018a). Steffens also toured with Marley for two weeks on invitation from Island Records on the Survival Tour (Steffens 2018a, xxi). Similarly, Jay Strausser of WRUV (Radio Voice of the University of Vermont), a college-based radio station in Burlington, Vermont, presented a show called *Trenchtown Rock* for fifteen years and toured with Bob Marley and The Wailers in New York when they played at Madison Square Garden in 1980 (Steffens 2018a).

As a result, radio interviews found in data online regarding the USA were from sources on specialist reggae shows, and not so much on the mainstream. A lot of these shows were hosted in the alternative realm of college radio; stations run on campuses largely by students.[11] Steffens confirmed this view to me:

> Almost all of the programs were on noncommercial, public, and college stations, staffed with fanatics who had to go to great lengths to find materials for their shows. And because Bob received almost no television coverage, radio was absolutely critical to Bob's breakthrough in America. (2018a)

Marley tried to have a greater impact on Black radio stations in the USA through the single 'Could You Be Loved' (Marley 1980). The USA represented the market he really wanted to break into (it was like the last frontier), and radio was the key medium to do this.

Sims started to work again with Marley on his U.S. tour in 1980. He struck a deal with New York Black urban music station WBLS (Where Black Listeners Stay Tuned). WBLS is part of the MBN (Mutual Black Network) established in 1972 as the first nationwide radio network aimed at African Americans (Mlaffs 2022). WBLS agreed to play 'Could You Be Loved' (Marley 1980) every hour of the day for three months in exchange for Bob Marley and The Wailers being the opening act for the Commodores at Madison Square Garden for a concert promoted by WBLS (Steffens 2018b, 372). Sims was also paid $80,000 by Marley to get 'major play' on every Black radio station in the USA by effectively buying airtime (Steffens 2018b, 373). The concert at Madison Square Garden did not exactly turn out as planned. Bob Marley and The Wailers played two sold-out nights as the support act, and at both shows, after they had finished, the audience thinned out for The Commodores (Steffens 2017b 376).

The next day Bob Marley collapsed while running in a park in New York. He played one more concert, in Pittsburgh at the Stanley Theatre, before flying to Miami for cancer treatment. He had tried to 'break' the U.S. market – with radio promotion playing a key part in the process – with a planned sixty-day tour opening for Stevie Wonder, which never happened.

It is unclear what $80,000 worth of hype actually 'buys' on mainstream radio. Aside from the extensive airplay, there is evidence of only one mainstream radio interview, on Radio 96 X Hot FM in Miami in September 1980. This was with host Steve Gilbert and is a lengthy interview, available in three parts online, which included a live phone-in. During this interview, Gilbert asks a number of naive questions, for example:

Gilbert: Is there any music older than reggae?

Marley: Music itself is old, you know.

Gilbert: Yeah, but, er, would you say reggae is one of the oldest forms of music?

Marley: The African nations? I don't think reggae is one of the oldest forms. Reggae is one of the more, newer form, you know. But it has African roots.

Gilbert: It has African roots, and it's developed –

Marley: Yeah.

Gilbert: How many records have you made?

Marley: A lot. (Gilbert 1980)

Hearing it, we realise Gilbert speaks in a fast, on-air, confrontational tone, while Bob Marley sounds laid-back and relaxed. Gilbert, sensing he has just asked a question live on air that has basically led nowhere, immediately changes to a line of inquiry that is shallow, and Marley responds simply by saying: 'A lot'. After this, Marley is compared to the Bee Gees in relative popularity in Jamaica and is even asked, 'do people recognise you when you walk down the street?' (Gilbert 1980) which does seem a 'dumbed-out' kind of question to be asking Bob Marley. This reflects how a mainstream radio host could not connect with him so superficiality was the option. A number of other people in the studio, not named, join the interview. They prod on with more questions about Marley's popularity, this time questioning being 'outside' (which presumably means outside of Jamaica):

> *Interviewer 2*: You got to realise that Bob, being outside, and with, er, er, some of the, er [*clearly nervous*], er, characteristics of his religion, which is, er, Rastafarianism, he is naturally going to be, people are going to notice him, he's got his dreadlocks.
>
> *Marley:* But most time we wear it up.
>
> *Interviewer 2:* Up in the hat?
>
> *Marley:* So you can't really see it.
>
> *Interviewer 2:* But when you walk down the streets in New York, maybe it's not Bob Marley they are thinking of. (Gilbert 1980)

That last statement stigmatises Marley in a pejorative manner as the strange, dreadlocked 'alien' in New York. What makes this interview different happens when the phone lines are opened for listeners to talk to Marley in person, and the rest of the interview is made up largely of callers asking questions. Aside from this mainstream interview in Miami and a number of college radio appearances, there were a number of interviews carried out in America by people involved with various Black media outlets. This did not often occur in other countries and is evident from as far back as 1973, when Marley gave one of his first interviews outside of Jamaica, with Wanda Coleman, a Los Angeles-based writer, poet, and activist. Many of these interviews give us detailed information about 'how to interview Marley'. They are nonjudgmental and less formal and were often done by media people reflecting forms of Black Consciousness. Coleman noted, for example, that she had trouble understanding Marley's Jamaican patois and he had trouble comprehending her Los Angeles Black slang. As she says: 'That night and into the next day, I spent sixteen hours poring over the tapes, doing my best to "translate" our awkward exchange' (Coleman 1973). It is not clear whether Coleman's interview with Marley was ever broadcast, but it did make the front page of the Los Angeles Free Press (Coleman 1973).

One of the most interesting people to interview Marley was Mumia Abu-Jamal (1979). Abu-Jamal is a celebrated Black writer and radio journalist who has spent the last thirty-eight years in prison after being 'convicted and sentenced to death in 1982 for the murder of Philadelphia police officer Daniel Faulkner, an incident which took place on 9 December 1981' (Campaign to bring Mumia Home 2022). Throughout the interview Jamal refers to Marley as 'brother' and focuses on issues of Black liberation, unemployment rates for Blacks in Philadelphia, Rastafari and the song 'War' by Marley. Abu-Jamal also characterises this interaction as an 'inner-view' rather than an 'interview' (Abu-Jamal 1979). This interview did not air on radio at the time, but excerpts of it appeared on Prison Radio, an online archive featuring podcasts from Mumia Abu-Jamal's archives (Prison Radio 2021). Marley's links with various Black and anti-racist movements in the USA were inevitable given his Rasta beliefs, and in turn these movements themselves could identify with Marley. Clearly these more in-depth interviews had a more conscious tone than the superficial mainstream radio interview mentioned previously in Miami.

Marley's last radio interview in the USA took the form of a phone-in conversation with Jay Strausser on WRUV-Burlington, Vermont, on 5 November, 1980. This interview covered a variety of topics, from Marley's early days with Coxsone Dodd, to touring in Europe, and his health. By this time, many rumors had circulated about Marley's battle with cancer. This was an informal interview, carried out by a Marley enthusiast keen to update the audience (Strausser 1980). The interview, carried out around the same time as the one in Jamaica on JBC Radio (Sinclair 1980), is less edgy, but Marley's voice has a different tone. Possibly, due to the spread of his cancer, Marley did phone interviews rather than appear in person. Sinclair's interview on JBC can be found in various guises online, all of which appear to be edited, lasting roughly forty-five seconds with a fade-out at the end giving what we hear as a feeling of incompleteness. In contrast, Strausser's interview is just over sixteen minutes long and becomes quite candid by the end, when the presenter asks Marley to make an on-air promotional announcement for him, which he agrees to do (Strausser 1980).

To conclude, in this verse it is visible that radio is complex, and as we have seen, it differs from place to place. In Jamaica, radio underrepresented reggae and Rastas for decades, and it could even be argued Bob Marley was seldom featured on radio; his overall presence was limited. The dominant force in British radio during the era in question was the BBC. In the USA, commercial radio, controlled by networks and other group owners, ruled the day. In each of these contexts, and with varying degrees of power and control, these different forms of radio represent a form of homogenised mainstreaming. Where and how Bob Marley was featured was different from place to place. In Jamaica, while he was referred to as Bob and interviews were less formal and better informed culturally, he only appeared on air in interview form a handful of times – something which I find surprising given his rise to fame in the 1970s. The British radio mainstream marginalised Marley. The only in-depth interview available online is David Rodigan on Capital Radio (1980), which happened completely by accident.[12] Ironically, the same person who accidentally stumbled upon an interview with Bob Marley, David Rodigan, would eventually resign from Kiss FM – London in 2012 after twenty-two years on air, over the way reggae music was 'marginalised' (Burrell 2012). Some things never change. Similarly, in the USA, college and Black community radio outlets with either reggae enthusiasts or forms of radical political consciousness welcomed Marley with enthusiasm. In the meantime, the commercial mainstream approached him with naive questions about fame and the way he looked. Additionally, evidence exists of how he was bypassed as not suitable as a mainstream artist (Maeder 2016; Grant 2011). A similar example exists of xenoglossophobia by the BBC in the John Tobler interviews, which, although aimed for BBC Radio, never made it on air.

These threads on exclusion strike me the most and feel like a revelation. Tobler mentioned that the BBC, based on their understanding of Marley's patois, shelved his three Marley interviews (Tobler 2018). John Peel recounted how Marley auditioned for the BBC, which turned him down. Peel does not say exactly when this happened, but, even if his story is merely allegorical, just the fact that he mentioned it in a documentary indicates something alarming about the British radio establishment in the early 1970s with regard to Bob Marley specifically and reggae in general (Marre 2011). Marley's presence as a guest on radio in Britain and the USA was limited. Even in Jamaica then, Bob Marley, up until the time of his death, was only partially represented on radio.

When I started this research, I expected to find many more radio-based interviews. In exploring what exists, my overall conclusion is that Marley was present, albeit in a limited way, but compared to many of his contemporary popstar peers, his presence on radio was also his absence.

NOTES

1. From the data I collected online, Bob Marley did eighteen radio interviews, seventeen of these were in Jamaica, Britain and USA. The remaining interview was in Australia.

2. These sites are *Voice of the Sufferers* (ReggaeLover 2004) and *Marley Arkives* (Midnight Raver 2011).

3. David Rodigan MBE OD (born 24 June 1951) is a British radio DJ who is known for his selections of reggae and dancehall music. He has played on stations including Radio London, Capital 95.8, Kiss 100, BBC Radio 1Xtra, BBC Radio 2, and BFBS Radio. Rodigan was one of the few people in Britain to interview Bob Marley on radio (Rodigan 2017).

4. This is significant considering Bob Marley's conversion to Rastafari in the late 1960s.

5. Danny Sims (1932–2011) was a US-based music producer, publisher, and promoter. He signed Marley to his first international publishing and recording contracts in 1968 (White 1983, 227).

6. Clyde McKenzie was the first general manager of Irie FM Radio and a significant person in the Jamaican music and media industry.

7. These two recorded live sessions were as follows: 1. Recorded: 1973-05-01. First Broadcast: 15 May 1973. Repeated: 24 July 1973, 14 July 1980, 11 June 1981, featured songs Slave Driver / Rasta Man / Concrete Jungle 2. Recorded: 1973-11-26. Broadcast: 25 December 1973. Repeated: 11 June 1981 Featured songs Kinky Reggae / Can't Blame the Youth / Get Up Stand Up (John Peel Wiki 2022).

8. Jo Maeder was the first female disc jockey and one of the first female Top 40 DJs in the USA (McCoy 2002, 105).

9. Maeder also said she tried to sell the interview to many syndicated mainstream radio stations, but nobody was interested. Then, some twenty years later, the interview was sold to the Marley Estate with Maeder 'making a nice return on my initial investment' (Maeder 2016).

10. Frank (Frankie) Crocker was one of the most significant figures in Radio Broadcasting in the USA who was behind the pioneering Black WBLS radio network (Barlow 1999).

11. College radio has a history in the USA that goes back to 1924. Estimates vary from four hundred and forty one (Radio Survivor 2020) to seven hundred (Sisario 2008) licensed college currently radio stations in the USA.

12. Rodigan shares the insight that the interview happened when he saw Marley, out of the blue, on a stairwell at Island Records and thought he would seize the opportunity by plucking up the courage to ask for an interview (Rodigan 2017, 7).

Verse Four

What the Papers Say

Imagine a hypothetical scenario. An alien from another planet lands on Earth. On arrival, they are given one hundred articles from magazines and newspapers about a singer from a Caribbean island. After reading the aforementioned documents, the alien forms a variety of opinions regarding Bob Marley – even prior to hearing his music. However, we are not all in the same position as the alien in our hypothetical scenario, and most of the time we have heard a singer's music and thus formed an opinion before reading about them. This hypothetical situation highlights the unique informative nature of print media in the 1970s. Print media only consisted of the written word and some photographs; there was no direct awareness of the actual sound of music. In contrast, television and radio possessed moving images and audio content. As a result, sometimes writing about music in print is often demeaned. 'Writing about music is like dancing about architecture' is a maxim used to express the futility of discussing music through written text (Brackett 2008, 157). It may also be employed as an argument for dismissing music criticism altogether (Adelaide and Attfield 2021, 210–12). During the 1970s, when music publications such as *New Musical Express* (*NME*), *Melody Maker*, and *Sounds* flourished, print media had a distinct significance. As Neil Spencer, former editor of *NME* says: 'that was the only place the music could happen in the media. The mainstream press weren't interested. There were two TV shows, and the radio was mostly tame (There were precious exceptions, like [influential DJ] John Peel's shows)' (Chui 2018).

However, all three media – radio, television and print – represented a more didactic and directive 'sit-back-and-be-told-culture' in that they filtered information (Gauntlett 2011, 8) and told the public what to think. By doing this they had acted as a significant 'gatekeeper' from the late 1950s (Toynbee 1993, 290). However, print media had distinct qualities. In terms of informational depth and rhetorical engagement, print media possesses a distinctive quality. In the 1970s, print media, and especially music magazines, were rich sources of criticism and information. Bob Marley was featured more in print media than in radio and television during this era, which serves as the chapter's general observation. Thus, print sources played a more edifying and qualitative role than other media platforms. In terms of the significance of print as a medium, it is also noteworthy that many of the authors who interviewed the singer became experts and specialist narrators on him.

Print, then, is the most significant source in terms of volume and coverage on Marley. Despite this, research on this area in general is limited. Another factor making the press unique is the key role that they played in media strategies, as replicated forms of representation in official press kits, and Island Records, to whom Marley was signed from 1972, were no exception to this rule. For example, in 1973 *The Bob Marley and The Wailers Catch A Fire Press Kit* released by the company was a twelve-page document made up entirely of press clippings from eight publications, mainly from the music press but also featuring a provincial newspaper *Leicester Mercury* with the vernacular headline 'Reggae as it really is – by the guvnors' (Voice of The Sufferers 2018). The Record Company was sitting on a goldmine in the form of positive press content. Selected print content could be reproduced easily and at low cost through photocopiers and short print runs. Obviously, television and radio content was not so flexible and easy to replicate. There is also a tautological element at play here. In other words, the use of edited and archival press materials to increase media attention was key to the enormity of Bob Marley's influence in the 1970s with enticing headlines in the aforementioned press-kit like *The Wailers – New Sound 400 Years Old (everything You Need to Know About Reggae)* originally by Sebastian Clarke for *Rock Magazine* in 1973 (Voice of The Sufferers 2018) and *The Wild Side of Paradise Steaming with the Rude Boys, the Rastas and Reggae* in *Rolling Stone*, July 1973 (Voice of The Sufferers 2018). How could Bob Marley and The Wailers go unnoticed? In this sense the tautological role of press promoting itself for further press was easier to use as a vehicle for the promotion of Bob Marley.

There are a number of problematic issues however with this content concerning access, origins, and finding source material. While a wealth of material exists online – on websites, as PDF files, and images, it was impossible to find the original magazines and newspapers, due to the limitations of the research. The material is also centred from sources in Britain, Jamaica, and North America. I have found some content from Italy, Japan, Australia, Germany, and New Zealand but this is sparse and makes for a limited sample in terms of global coverage. It would have been good to find a record of printed material from Bob Marley's visits to Africa, notably Gabon, Ethiopia, and Zimbabwe. Only one interview was found from his trip to Gabon, which was conducted in French via an interpreter and it is not clear if this was ever published (Bob Marley Concerts 2021). While some visual content exists, including the video footage of the historic Zimbabwe Independence Celebrations in 1980 there is no evidence of textual print media coverage available online. Moreover, one of the most disappointing ellipses on content concerns USA Black 'lifestyle' magazines, such as *Essence* and *Ebony*, which regrettably are not available online either.[1] In addition, although there is a wealth of information available from music magazines at the Rocks Backpages website (Hoskyns 2000), this is only accessible through a paid subscription, and the articles are only reproduced in text format. Despite the reality that discovering this resource was a revelation, it was unfortunate not to be able to look at the original articles together with any visual content and original layout and typography.

Analysing printed texts also required a different methodological framework, due to the volume of texts collected, which number several hundred through online data and my own collection of original sources. Out of these I focused on a sample of a hundred. Due to the limitations of my research, it was impossible to examine everything as that requires a separate book solely on print media. In addition, many of these texts contained a variety of less pertinent factual information, such as concert listings, advertisements, and brief mentions. Instead, I concentrated on in-depth interviews, album reviews, and features, of which I analysed a hundred in depth from a variety of sources using document analysis as a type of qualitative research in which the researcher interprets documents to give voice and meaning on a specific topic (Bowen 2009). Similar to the analysis of focus group or interview transcripts, document analysis incorporates coding content into themes (Bowen 2009).

What intrigued me most about the print content was the range of representations and the quantity of material; from mainstream publications to more specialist music magazines. Due to the variety of content, I discovered that document analysis provided the ability to analyse things and classify broad topics by creating codes and specific themes. Based on a sample of a hundred print texts, a coding tree was created for the analysis and is available for viewing online as Diagram 1. Bob Marley Printed Press Coding Tree (Hajimichael 2022). The purpose of the coding tree is not quantitative, that is, to count the frequency of themes in the sample, but rather to consider these themes from a semiotic perspective as factors that contributed to audiences reading the text and forming opinions about the topic. Before expanding on this at length, I would like to introduce the coding analysis by explaining a few key things. Due to the large number of themes and subcategories found, this study will primarily concentrate on the first two: 'Code 1 Critique' and 'Code 2 Personal Life' (Hajimichael 2022). This is so for two basic reasons. The volume of information in these two codes was deemed more pertinent to the present research. In addition, I intend to investigate 'Code 3 Unique Events and Themes' in a separate study due to the historical significance of several Bob Marley concerts in 1980.[2] In addition, it is vital to study the many forms and categories of Bob Marley-related printed press content, in part to comprehend the range of content and in part to conceptualise what people were actually doing when they wrote about him. Clearly, a substantial portion of the printed material constitutes a body of work by writers who were seen as key 'gatekeepers', primarily working in the music press, and many of these in the 1970s featured extensive Bob Marley coverage. Consequently, I believe it is important to consider some background regarding these sources.

PRINTED PRESS – FACTUAL BACKGROUND INFORMATION

The most influential of these were Anglophone publications in the UK and USA. Magazines such as *New Musical Express* (*NME*), *Sounds*, and *Melody Maker*, came out on a weekly basis in the UK. *NME* reached a circulation of three hundred thousand by 1973 (Hearsam 2013). *Sounds* was one of the first music papers to cover punk rock music (Bushell 2016). *Melody Maker*, founded in 1926, was the oldest British music paper, and by 1970 it reached over one million weekly sales (Melody Maker 1970).

In the USA *Crawdaddy* was 'the first magazine to take rock and roll seriously' (Rockwell 1976). It was published monthly and preceded *Rolling Stone* and *Creem*. The tenth edition of *Crawdaddy* had just under twenty thousand sales (Willis 2002). *Creem*, another monthly magazine in the USA, was one of the first outlets where the term 'punk rock' was used, as far back as the May 1971 issue. It had a circulation of just over two hundred thousand magazines by 1976, which was second only to *Rolling Stone* (Rubin 2020). The biweekly *Rolling Stone,* founded in 1967 in San Francisco, came out of and reported on hippie counter-culture. Ironically, out of all the magazines mentioned, it is the only one still in circulation. In 1974, the magazine had a circulation of over three hundred thousand. By 1998 this increased to over a million (Umberger n.d.). Another US magazine, more industry-oriented and influential, is *Billboard.* Founded in 1894 as a trade magazine for bill posters, it became more music-centred with the rise in popularity of phonographic records, radio, and jukeboxes (Annad 2006).

So far, the focus has been on mainstream music publications which featured Bob Marley, but what about more specialist publications? These were more focused on genres like R'n'B, jazz, and reggae, as well as specific subjects like legalizing marijuana. *Black Music,* published in Britain, and *Swing* magazine from Jamaica, are the most notable examples of niche publications I came across from the 1970s.

Black Music was first published in 1973 as a monthly magazine. Reading its features on reggae in general and Marley in specific gave a different type of insight, particularly those by writer Carl Gayle, a pioneering Black British journalist. Johnny Golding published *Swing* in Jamaica on a monthly basis. Regrettably, I could only find one issue of this online.

A final area of content concerns the broadsheets, the dailies, and magazines considered 'mainstream' media but not writing just about music. As Marley's fame increased, with time he attracted more mainstream attention in newspapers such as *The Daily Mirror* and *The Guardian* in Britain, and in *Playboy* and *The New York Times* in the USA. While it is tempting to classify this content as just mainstream, it is not doing justice to qualitative differences between writers who wrote about Marley. Neil Spencer's features in *The Guardian* have radically different nuances to other mainstream newspapers. Let us now turn to the in-depth thematic findings.

CODE 1: CRITIQUE – POSITIVE/NEGATIVE REVIEWS

People had much to say about Bob Marley in terms of critique, with opinions ranging from positive to negative regarding LP releases, live concert reviews, and features. I guess this is unavoidable given the 1970s was an era of interpretation and individual expression in the music press. It is difficult to analyse this comprehensively, and frankly, the veracity of opinions on Marley was anticipated, whether they were centred on albums, live reviews, or in-depth interviews. A crucial argument in this chapter is that it is unwise to attempt to categorise the diverse ways in which people have written about Marley. However, some articles stand out exceptionally, for different reasons. The negativity of Nick Kent, who wrote acerbic content for *NME,* is notable during the opening lines of his interview with Marley where he confesses 'IT'S LIKE this, see: I just don't like reggae music' (Kent 1977). Why a publication would send a journalist to interview a musician whose music they loathe is odd. The truth is that Nick Kent, a by-product of the whole Punk Rock era as a writer, was the story, not the artist. From a different kind of angle, but more stoic on Rastafari and Marley's selling power, Simon Frith wrote: 'I am interested to know what white audiences are drawing from reggae (and I don't believe it has much to do with white guilt – none of this music feeds my masochism)'. He also adds Marley's 'righteousness is founded in our (white) unrighteousness' (Frith 1976). There is an additional name-check in the same article through reference to Carl Gayle 'who draw(s) something different' from The Wailers' music (through being Black). Gayle was one of the first writers to specialise in reggae in the UK. Some of his output is ethnographic, particularly the six-page report on the reggae underground (Gayle 1974). Frith's insight, though, on how writing about reggae, audiences, and 'race' is significant in its frankness.

There were also a wide range of opinions on Marley releases, from favourable to heavy critique. *Exodus* (1977a) for example was generally received in a positive way. Vivien Goldman proclaims in the opening line of a review, 'From a purely marketing point of view, this is the one' (Goldman 1977). Simultaneously, on the other side of the Atlantic, Griel Marcus observed about the same release: 'The more I listen to this album, the more I am seduced by the playing of the band; at the same time, the connection I want to make with the music is subverted by overly familiar lyric themes unredeemed by wit or color, and by the absence of emotion in Marley's voice' (Marcus 1977). Reading a review like this, it does make me wonder, did we listen to the same album? Emotionally, *Exodus* (1977a) is Marley at his finest creatively and conceptually.

Similar dichotomies exist on other releases. Charlie Gillet questioned *Catch a Fire* (1973a) as: 'Reggae is a deep beat and melodies you can't forget, where Catch a Fire is a soft beat and guitar solos you heard before and were glad to have forgotten' (Gillet 1973). Richard Williams, a year earlier, in his lengthy and more ethnographic piece took a completely different stance, hailing the LP as 'better than any of his previous output' (Williams 1972).

CODE 1 – MAINSTREAMING EXAMPLE

Mainstreaming of music can take many forms, and in the practice of music journalism it often relies on comparing a music from the 'fringe' (in this case reggae by Bob Marley from post-colonial Jamaica) through a number of analogies with artists in the 'mainstream' of pop and rock of that era. One reason why writers did this in the 1970s was to make Marley's music more digestible to 'mainstream' audiences. *Playboy* is possibly one of the last places I would have expected to find an article on Bob Marley in 1976; largely because the singer is incompatible aesthetically, culturally, and politically with the publication. The following description is definitive of *Playboy* – 'What Hefner did was, in one way, as old as sex itself: he took the heterosexual male gaze and commodified it' (Gopnik 2017). Understandably, Marley's success by 1976 resulted in much more mainstream coverage. *Playboy* fits this category. By the end of the seventies the USA magazine had a circulation of around six million (Encyclopaedia of Chicago, n.d.).

The article in *Playboy,* written as an editorial review, discusses a 1976 concert at the Beacon Theatre in New York City as part of The Rastaman Vibration Tour (*Playboy* 1976). It is located under the music section of the magazine with no author credit. The review is more mainstream, even naive in its approach. The author uses four analogies in three columns equating Marley with 'Rock stars' including a sweeping opening statement which declares 'Let's say this right up front and underline it twice: Bob Marley and The Wailers seem finally to have emerged as the finest rock-'n'- roll band of the Seventies . . . (*Marley is*) right up there up with any of the giants you might care to name Chuck Berry through Sly Stone. And that includes the Beatles, Otis Reading, the Stones all of them. That's how good they are' (*Playboy* 1976, 34). It is hard to imagine such a diversity of musical icons of that era all being homogenised in this way. A definitive statement on reggae also follows as the 'slow fire, sensuous, exotic, yet always familiar, for one of its parents is our own rock 'n' roll' (1976, 34). Marley is cast as 'skinny in the classic mode of rock-star skinniness (Dylan, Jagger)' (1976, 34). The Jagger analogy was also found in another article with the title 'Bob Marley Is the Jagger of Reggae' (Carr 1973).

The *Playboy* article concludes 'There is a terrible f*****g tidal wave building in the Third World, and Marley is its prophet' (*Playboy* 1976, 35). This led me to even assume perhaps Hugh Hefner wrote the piece. As for a description of the concerts themselves, which after all, was the article's main intent, we are merely informed 'To be fair, it should be added the two sold-out shows we caught at New York City's Beacon Theatre there performances were not equally fine, the Friday night one seeming to sag in the middle' (*Playboy* 1976, 34–35).

Reading the review, I wondered if it was about Marley. Mainstreaming him as a 'skinny rock star' playing 'sensuous exotic' music which can only really be comprehended based on mainly 'rock' references demeans the quality and depth of Marley's messages and rooted perspectives. What I found more alarming than the review itself was that it was essentially replicated, more or less (with the expletive f-word edited out at the end) in Jamaica under the lazily adapted title 'Reggae – musical tidal wave . . . Bob Marley the "prophet"' (*The Daily Gleaner* 1976). Perhaps we can call this journalistic plagiarism or maybe it is not, as there is an opening reference that the report was taken from *Playboy* (*The Daily Gleaner* 1976). The Jamaican newspaper was, in a sense, trying to indicate how far Marley was progressing. What does disturb me is that it was included without any kind of critique, because clearly the inaccuracies of *Playboy* and the 'mainstreaming' of Marley is highly problematic. Both articles can be accessed online and are worth a view (Hajimichael 2022).

CODE 1 – WRITING AS ETHNOGRAPHY

Following on from these differences of opinion and mainstreaming, the most important aspect of critique thematically relates to ideas around what some key writers were actually doing epistemologically. This theme centres on the idea that writing about music is more than 'dancing about architecture'; it is actually a form of ethnographic engagement, which has been touched on already, but I want to consider it now more at length. The music journalist in this sense becomes a key conveyor of 'thick' or detailed description in an ethnographic sense, and by being there, in Jamaica, as an avid 'outside observer'. I would go so far as to argue that this became a press 'tradition' early on.

Vivien Goldman's account, for example, of the assassination attempt on Bob Marley's life, gives us graphic details of a very violent crime by someone who was there. It also provides an in-depth analysis of the Machiavellian characteristics of Jamaican sectarian politics (Goldman 2006). Lester Bangs' frank and lengthy article on a mission to interview Bob Marley tells us just as much about the singer as it does about a variety of aspects of the surroundings, the history of Jamaica and its 'colonial hangover' (Bangs 2004).[3] The article also provides valuable human dynamics between journalists and artists, as well as between the interviewer and interviewee. In this notable piece of writing, which reads like a witty academic field diary at times, Bangs tells us of a journalist from a mainstream US publication struggling to interview Bob Marley because he did not understand his accent. This indeed becomes a recurring theme in many print-based interviews. Misinterpretation may have resulted in misleading information on what the artist may have said. Marley sometimes appeared frustrated by the manner in which journalists questioned him about petty matters, as Bangs explains: 'Davis asked Bob what he thought about people coming down to ask all these questions. "Well", said Bob, "as long as dem get da right understanding of da answers and write it . . . because plenty time, plenty guys just write for kicks, y'know, like jus' turn in a joke ting is goin' on, an is serious ting . . ."' (Bangs 2004, 66).

The issue of language appears again here. This time Marley stresses it is important that he is understood. Marley was not amused by a certain recent interview in which a writer from New York asked him questions like 'Where did you get your jeans'? and 'When you were in New York, did you go shopping at Bloomingdale's'? (Bangs 2004, 66).

Writers writing for 'kicks' also echoes the idea that many journalists did not even know what they were doing in Jamaica interviewing Marley. Bangs candidly encounters one such person at the hotel in the presence of Chris Blackwell. The journalist writes for *Rolling Stone* and is not named but Bangs dubs him as 'Gonzo'.

> By the pool I met my colleague from *Rolling Stone,* and over drinks Blackwell asked him what angle he was going to approach his story from. 'Oh, I dunno, man', he replied, with no idea who he was talking to, 'I'm just gonna use the gonzo approach for this one pretty much. I intend to do my whole story from the poolside bar and go out of the hotel as little as possible. I mean, who gives a fuck, y'know? I'm just in this for the free drinks and to see if I can get laid'.
>
> Blackwell looked a little green around the eyeballs, but went on to ask Gonzo what he thought of reggae.
>
> 'I can't remember ever hearing any. The last album I really got into was The Allman Brothers Live at Fillmore East. Hell, man, I don't even have a record player!' Blackwell's jaw dropped. (Bangs 2004, 72)

This is a humorous example of Bangs' own unique brand of 'gonzo journalism' and it certainly indicates how out of touch specific journalists were at the time. Imagine if 'Gonzo', as Bangs calls him, had to conduct an interview with Marley? Additional examples of ethnographic content exist in articles by Vivien Goldman and Chris Salewicz. The titles of many of Goldman's articles indicate the writer was often in the right place at the right time. An example of this is 'Bob Marley in His Own Backyard' – a lengthy interview in the singer's home in Kingston, Jamaica, where he talks about his beliefs comprehensively (Goldman 1979). 'One Love Peace Festival' is a review of the historic peace concert where Marley called opposing political leaders, Michael Manley and Edward Seaga, on stage for a symbolic handshake. Bob Marley and Peter Tosh, two of the founding Wailers, performed separate sets at the concert. *Sounds* featured a really detailed account of this historic Jamaican event (Goldman 1978b). Chris Salewicz's 'A Day at the Gun Court' (1979) provides a spine chilling reflection on being inside the notorious prison set up in 1974 by parliament to judge criminal cases involving firearms without a jury ('Gun Court Act' 1974). After leaving 'Gun Court' Marley smiles at the writer and states: 'There, you're the first journalist ever to go inside the Gun Court' (Salewicz 1979).

An interrelated sub-theme within the 'ethnography' theme is a subject I will loosely call 'language issues – understanding Marley' which we just touched on (Bangs 2004, 66). This has two main aspects. The first aspect relates to journalists struggling to understand Marley during press interviews, and at the same time, specific journalists reflecting on the issue of language as a form of critique aimed at their counterparts. With regard to the second aspect, I will explore it more in the next sub-section on beliefs as it can even be viewed as a kind of auto-ethnography on journalism. With regard to the first aspect however, I feel a sense of writers being out of their depth, and it feels naive on their part that they made such blatant confessions on not understanding Bob Marley. Pete Silverton for example confesses:

> No interview that I'd read had ever captured either the force of his religious obsession or the fact that whole chunks of his spiel were almost incomprehensible – not only because of the accent – and rambling to a point where, at his frequent interjections of 'seen', all I could do was nod helplessly and hope I could make sense of it when I played the tape back later. (Silverton 1978)

Charles Shaar Murray was equally candid about his language deficiency when interviewing Marley: 'I'm not sure if he's misunderstood the question or if I've misunderstood the answer or both' (Murray 1978).

In an interview with Roger Steffens, I quizzed him on this point from a generic perspective, particularly if he felt some journalists who interviewed Marley possibly did not understand him:

> Well, yes I think you are right there and there is evidence of this sometimes when journalists make those kind of naïve confessions and I think it happened on a number of occasions. For me though it has always been important to understand people but at the same time it does feel like a sort of fifty-fifty type of engagement sometimes. (Steffens 2018a)

Another take on this is perhaps that language is something Bob Marley toyed with depending on who was interviewing him. Journalist Kris Needs hints at this through the following observation: 'I'm so thankful that, contrary to legend, he isn't employing the dense patois he notoriously calls up when he doesn't trust a journalist (having said that, several sentences do trail into Trenchtown-speak that proves impossible to transcribe next day)' (Needs 2017).

Concurrently, there is evidence that this naiveté extends to Bob Marley's beliefs, which I will now discuss.

CODE 1 – BELIEFS

There are notable differences between ethnographic and acerbic accounts regarding Marley's beliefs. Many writers attempted to explain Rastafarian beliefs to non-Rasta audiences. A lengthy interview by Steve Davis (aka Stephen Davis) with Marley featured in *JahUgliman,* a magazine published by Carl Gayle, reads like a raw data ethnographic engagement (Davis 1980). We find references to biblical quotes and what the writer terms as a 'mystical semi-secret organization of Rastas in Jamaica called The Twelves Tribes of Israel' with Marley confirming 'True. Me is a member of that organization. Me name Joseph. The revelation of the Bible. We are the 12,000 people who know we are of the tribe of Judah' (Davis 1980). At the other extreme, Pete Silverton proclaims negativity towards Haile Selassie: 'Okay, so Jah has given a lot of Jamaicans a sense of pride, a consciousness of their own intrinsic worth. But, I ask you, back to Africa? Hailie Selassie as a living God when he's six feet under donating his vital organs to the worms' (Silverton 1978).

Inevitably, this was not stated during the interview (in Marley's presence) but as a rhetorical after thought by the writer, perhaps to make his article appeal more to the stereotypical appeal of a 'non-Rasta' audience. The area where there seems however to be less difference concerning Marley's beliefs concerns marijuana. Many writers could not really grasp the significance of marijuana to Rastas. I get the impression they were simply shocked by how much Bob Marley smoked. Take this comment for instance: 'Hey Bob, while we're on the subject of 'erb, how come you can put away such a colossal amount of the stuff and still manage to stay upright, let alone play football, put on a dynamite show an' t'ing? Most people I know wander around in circles with their eyes crossed and then fall over if they smoke that much' (Murray 1978). However, a more reasoned connection on weed and reggae, and how their vital linkage in a Jamaican context may have given writers a different outline. Marijuana plays such a central role in reggae, to demean and trivialise it, is missing a fundamental element of a specific belief system:

> The sociocultural perceptions of and responses to marijuana/weed, particularly among Jamaica's underclasses, are encoded in the country's popular music, which has historically emanated primarily from this group. As such, the weed/marijuana is celebrated by Jamaican musicians, particularly in the rocksteady, reggae and dancehall genres, as the holy herb, the religious sacrament, the meditation herb, the wisdom weed, the 'natural' or organic herb, the panacea for all aliments, the calmer, the adrenaline pusher and the aphrodisiac, among other labels. (Hope 2013, 344)

It follows then that 'weed' was integral to Marley's philosophy. Something he stood up for and defended so much so that, according to writer Penny Reel, the singer refused to perform at Admiral Ken's Bouncing Ball Club in Peckham, London, in 1973, because the club's manager took down the promotional posters due to their 'weed' content.

> The Wailers reach and set up onstage. Seco arranges his percussion tableau, Family Man takes his bass from its case. Bob arrives and immediately notices the missing posters. On hearing the reason why, he declares that a club that

refuses to display the poster on its wall is a club that he, Bob Marley, refuses to grace with his presence. Upon which, he leaves. (Reel 2003)

When it came to how he wished to be portrayed through media, in this case promotional posters for the album *Catch a Fire* (1973a), Marley steadfastly refused to make any concessions, which speaks volumes about his philosophies and beliefs. Concerning how the singer wanted to be represented, I believe this is important to keep in mind. He could have easily accepted the venue manager's decision by accepting this act of censorship. Marley, however, stood firm and did not sing that night. Neil Spencer argues that many people who interviewed Marley scrutinised his beliefs without really understanding them. Writing a moving obituary after the singer's death from cancer in 1981, the former *NME* editor made the following observation:

> He was made to suffer in the interviews for his adherence of Rasta dogma though few of his attackers possessed the underlying spirituality that animated his beliefs. The present writer remembers seeing Marley under attack in a German hotel from prosaic German radio interviewers pressing home questions about Haile Selassie's bank account.
>
> 'Why you no check the heart that beat instead of the bank account'? he answered, and it seemed then that whatever his failings Marley was more on the side of life than the grey rationalists who pursued him. (Spencer 1981)

Spencer's reflection represents a form of critique to his contemporaries in music journalism which is an admirable trait. He highlights a form of bad practice, which is noticeable in numerous interview situations, across a range of media. It is however interesting that these kinds of reflections are being made by print journalists.

CODE 2: SUCCESS – FROM COUNTRY BOY TO WORLDWIDE ICON

Moving onto the second set of codes, success is an interesting and multifaceted thematic covered in different ways by the printed press. Factually, there is no doubt that during Marley's short life span, he experienced substantial upward social mobility. The narrative of the 'country boy' coming to the sprawling urban mass of Kingston and eventually developing into a worldwide popular music icon exists in many news stories and features. Perhaps these fascinations in the press started from the fact that this social mobility puzzled people, and that somehow Marley, with fame and fortune, had changed. The following exchange in *Circus* exemplifies this:

What about the money he's making? Marley is asked. Reporters have pointed out that the star owns a fancy BMW automobile, and his explanation that the brand name stands for Bob Marley and the Wailers has done little to get them off his case. 'Rastafari is the king of kings, Rastafari is the creator, so why defend a car. I mean, f**k a kee-yar, we don't even want car, we want our own freedom; that is more than car and truck and boat and plane and house. (Schruers 1978)

Many media writers quizzed Marley on his success and the contradiction of being a militant Rasta singer and a successful artist. In the one interview he gave to *Tg2* in Italy in 1980 he responded in the following way to a provocative question regarding the potential contradiction between the message of his songs and the earnings from the sale of his records: 'The money is not important, it is only important for the white man. He made a religion. What matters is God, the sky, the earth, the sun, nature. Therefore, money does not count for anything, it is just pieces of paper and should not affect life' (Daniele and Venditti 2021).

Success, money, and fame however, regardless of how defiant or humble Marley's responses were to these subjects, brought an increased sense of mythologization.

CODE 2 – MYTHOLOGIZATION

It is often quoted that Marley was the first 'third world' artist to conquer the 'first world', that he was a 'Rasta prophet' (Terrell 2004), and that he had acquired 'almost messianic proportions' (Bradshaw 1984). This is what writers in magazines said about the singer in their articles after interviewing him. Marley did not say these things about himself, but during his lifetime, as he became more famous, his stature increased and he became in a sense, more sanctified. The idea however of the artist from the 'third' world conquering the 'first' contradicted his own views. Having researched hundreds of printed articles available online I have yet to find any sign of the singer as boastful, egocentric, or blowing his own trumpet about his success. Marley's own view on his iconic status is interesting. In *Smash Hits,* a largely pop publication, Mike Stand quizzes him on this:

> It's no wonder he's become a hero and an inspiring figurehead. But when I suggested this to him, he waved the idea aside as if it was far too pompous to have anything to do with him:
> 'No, music is the one that is the hero. We help the music. It is the universal language and we carry a certain message. But Jamaican people not look on you as "star". Them have love an' respec' an' t'ing. To tell you the trut' I am not enormous person, me just a man o' the ghetto'. (Stand 1980)

Accordingly, from his inception as an artist signed to a significant record label, Marley's media persona was strategised through a number of accolades that inflated his humble status. Even as far back as 1973, Richard Williams' teasing title asked the question 'Bob Marley: The First Genius of Reggae' (Williams 1973). Marley's music was described as a 'tidal wave' from the 'third world' (*Playboy* 1976). He was also 'the apocalyptic soul rebel' (Cohen 1975). All these descriptive narratives created an inflated version of Bob Marley. The ground for the fertilisation of Marley's mythical status was well prepared through the music press in the 1970s, and while this is going to be discussed more at length in Verse Six, it is worth emphasizing here that without all of this content, which at times borders on the hyperbolic, the marketing of Marley could have taken a radically different course. Exaggeration also comes into his mythical status, mainly after his passing, on the causes of his death from cancer. While these stories and rumours are not so evident in media content during the 1970s, they came out more initially in biographies (post-1980s) and as online articles during the 'fake news era' (post-2014). The story that carried most resonance concerned an alleged 'plot' by the CIA to assassinate Bob Marley which I will address more later on with regard to 'myths' peddled after he passed away in 1981.

CODE 2: FAMILY AND PERSONAL LIFE

Obviously, while this thematic became more dominant after this death, particularly in biographic texts and with intricate detail (White 1983), aspects of Marley's personal and family life were also mentioned in the press in the 1970s, but often in a way that was just in passing and descriptive. Richard Williams for example states:

> HE WAS BORN in Kingston, Jamaica, the son of a white British Army captain from Liverpool – 'I only remember seeing him twice, when I was small' – and a black Jamaican who wrote spirituals and sang in the local Apostolic Church. Unlike most half-castes, who violently take one side or another, it's given him an unusually open view of race: 'I don't really check people's colour', he says. (Williams 1973)

However, this theme was not as dominant. The same can be said of personal relationships and Marley's views on the convention of marriage. However, when Marley was referred to on the front page of the British tabloid *The Daily Mirror* things were exceptionally different. In the first of two sensationalised articles on the relationship between Cindy Breakspeare – who at the time had recently been crowned 'Miss World' – and Bob Marley (Steffens 2018b,

198), the tabloid uses the headline 'MISS WORLD'S WILD MAN' with the subheading 'I have nine children by seven girls, he claims' (Ricketts and Dowdney 1976). Of course these statements are made on Marley's behalf, he did not actually talk to the tabloid. There is also a claim that he plans to divorce his legal wife, Rita Marley, who is not named, but predictably we are not told of the source of this claim (Ricketts and Dowdney 1976). The front also features two photos. Cindy Breakspeare on the left, smiling to the camera in a casual summer dress, 'The Beauty Queen' and Bob Marley in an equally sized image on the right of the article, shot as a close up singing live on the microphone playing the guitar, framed as 'The Wild Man' (Ricketts and Dowdney 1976). A few days later, a second article appears, again on the front page. It's important to note that in between the two articles, something seismic had happened; a group of gunmen raided Bob Marley's home on the night of 3 December 1976, in an attempt to kill him and members of his entourage. The second article has the headline: 'MISS WORLD GOES INTO HIDING', with the subtitle 'Cindy slips away to her wild man of pop' (Gibbs 1976). According to the newspaper 'friends' close to Breakspeare, (note these 'friends' are not named – so assumedly this is based on gossip) said she was 'desperately missing Marley and has flown to a secret rendezvous in the sun to meet him' and that 'she was terribly upset about the recent gun raid on his Kingston home. Marley, who claims to have nine children by seven women, was wounded in the arm'. The tabloid also adds 'She [Cindy Breakspeare] refused to discuss Marley the black cult leader and wild man of rock' (Gibbs 1976).

All of these distortions indicate how exaggerated a mainstream reportage was on the singer. None of the information is given a credible source, and it could simply be read as something concocted to sell on a topical subject. In no other print matter have I found such fabrications. This takes us back to a finding towards the end of the previous chapter on radio. The more mainstream the media coverage, the more trivialised, and in this case, offensive, it becomes. The 'black cult leader' (a trivialised exaggeration of Marley and Rastafari) and 'wild man' are intentionally biased discourses. These create more rigid meanings as a news-feed in line with a *Daily Mirror* mainstream readership/audience. Both articles are available for viewing online (Hajimichael 2022).

CODE 2 – SHOOTING – EXILE

On 3 December 1976, a group of gunmen forcefully entered Bob Marley's home at fifty-six Hope Road in Kingston, Jamaica, and opened fire with automatic weapons. Vivien Goldman, who was in Jamaica at the time, writes a spine chilling account of what happened (2006, 103–109). Obviously such a tumultuous event made the front pages of the newspaper in Jamaica, including graphic photos of Marley immediately after the shooting with a bloodstained shirt pointing how the bullet had gone through his arm. The same image was also made into a t-shirt and the incident inspired an award winning book decades later (James 2015). The two are linked in an interesting article (Cocozza 2015). While the Jamaican press featured the shooting as their lead stories on 4 December 1976, it took a day or two for things to filter to other places around the world. One short *United Press International* (*UPI*) piece even included the misleading headline 'Jamaican Singer Is Killed' but then in its opening sentence confirms 'Bob Marley, one Jamaica's top reggae singers, and three members of his troupe were shot and wounded Friday night by a band of gunmen who raided his home' (Midnight Raver 2012c).

There is noticeably a different kind of coverage from mainstream international press. Articles found were brief, and at times, like the previous *UPI* example, misleading; *The Ottawa Journal,* for instance, a few days after the shooting, when Marley appeared at the Smile Jamaica Concert opens with the line 'Jamaican rock star Bob Marley gave a free concert here, two days after he was hit by unidentified snipers' (Learyfan 2016). Additionally, on the same online thread, cuttings from several other press agencies indicate they shared the same story, 'copy-paste' style. It is important to note a descriptive difference here. Many of the international news agencies used language like 'snipers' which is a word not used in the Jamaican press. It also gives a different kind of emotive impression as to how the shooting took place.

There is no clear explanation for the shooting attempt on Bob Marley's life. It remains a mystery and has not been fully investigated, even to this day. However, the shooting, although extensively featured at length in the press in Jamaica, and more marginally covered by the international print outlets, would become the biggest mystery to follow Marley through many future media engagements. Nonetheless it iss integral in the process of mythologizing the incident through a meticulously distorted conspiracy theory. For decades to come, biographers, writers, and in a more contemporary sense, bloggers on the net – who are too many to list – have exhausted this 'story' extensively. Eventually the reasons behind the shooting have become an 'urban myth' because of various links made with local political parties in Jamaica and the US Central Intelligence Agency (CIA). Due to the prevalence of this issue in television interviews, it will be covered in greater depth in Verse Five. In front of the cameras, questions about the shooting would torment Marley for the remainder of his life. On a multitude of websites, the same troubling themes continue to be posed in the form of fake news stories. These are frequently based on 'unofficial sources' (Tapalaga 2022) and several debunked myths. The most infamous is that of ex-CIA employee Bill Oxley, who admitted to killing Bob Marley on his deathbed. This has since been archived on the web due to its falsity (Dmitry 2017).

CODE 2 – CANCER – DEATH – FUNERAL

Obviously, the subject of Marley's cancer diagnosis, treatment, death, funeral, and deification is possibly the most covered in terms of press content in specific and media content in general. As a thematic issue, this coverage is diverse and follows a certain timeline. Indeed, the chronology of the singer's illness, death, and funeral in terms of print media is possibly a chapter in itself, when one takes into account the volume of content. There is a parallel narrative on Marley's initial cancer diagnosis which is divided between information that was initially 'private' but would come out in biographic work after his death (White 1983; Davis 1983; Taylor and Henry 2003). Much of the information on Marley's health started to emerge publicly through print media reports in 1977, following a toe injury sustained in a soccer match in Paris (Steffens 2018b, 274). However, at the time, the extent of his injury was not clear from any of the actual media coverage. After Paris, he played a series of amazing live shows at The Rainbow Theatre in North London, Britain. The extent of Marley's medical condition emerged more publicly through media reports later on in November 1977. In an interview with Marley in Miami, USA, for *Rolling Stone*, after touring in Europe and taking a few months off to recover from the toe injury, we are given the following information:

> It's been a strange year for Bob Marley. He recently underwent surgery to remove a tumor from the big toe on his right foot. It had been feared that the medical problem might end Marley's performing career, but the surgery was successful and it now appears he'll be back onstage next year. (Swenson 1977)

Even so, this is the only detail provided about Marley's illness and at the end of the article the writer proclaims:

> And, in fact, his religion may have aided his swift recovery from the operation. The Rasta diet avoids salt, meat and alcohol and is said to promote excellent health. 'Bob will be in good shape for many years', Don Taylor (*Marley's Manager*) noted, 'because he's so disciplined about his diet. He'd rather go hungry than eat the wrong kind of food'. (Swenson 1977)

It is clear from the singer's tour schedule that from 4 June 1977, the last night at The Rainbow, until the One Love Peace Concert in Jamaica in April 1978, he did no live shows, presumably due to his injury, operation, and recuperation (Concert Archives 2022). However, from April 1978 until 23 September 1980 at The Stanley Theatre Pittsburgh, Marley toured the globe relentlessly, criss-crossing continents: America, Africa, Europe, Asia, and Australasia. Indeed 1978 and 1979 were the singer's busiest years tour wise, with forty-eight and fifty-two concerts respectively followed by thirty-nine in 1980 (Concert Archives 2022). Statistically speaking, this is just under one hundred and forty out of his total of two hundred and seventy live concerts (between 1972 and 1980). This represents 51 percent of all his concerts during those years (Concert Archives). Furthermore, all of this happened during the three years after he was initially diagnosed with cancer in his toe. In an interview conducted by Basil Wilson and Herman Hall at Essex House in May 1978, published in the June/July 1978 issue of *Everybody's Magazine*, Bob Marley comes across as a very angry figure.[4] This is not something found anywhere else in other media from that time, such as television or radio. The article is worth quoting at length:

Everybody's: Are you definitely touring the States this year?

Marley: Yes, we are going to do a tour. Physically I am alright but there is some little bullshit that going on that I don't like. The business that I am in, I must know everything and if I don't know everything, I don't work. See.

Everybody's: Is that the problem with the North American tour?

Marley: Here what happen now. What happen to them is that they do not want to run this thing like how I want to run it. Them want to run me on a star trip but I am not on any star trip. I want that any time I tour Europe and I look at myself and realise that my structure (health) run down, I must rest. But they are not concerned with my structure. They run and plan a North American tour. You must remember when I was in Europe, you don't even drink water. You have to purposely drink water and when you finish that tour, they set up another tour. I watch Muhammad Ali and Alan Cole (ref needed) and I see how these athletes take care of their structure. But the people who set up the tour do not work. They just collect money and when night come, you find them in bed with two girls while you 'bus' your r…e.. and a work hard all the time. When my toe was injured, they didn't even know. My toe nail had just come out and when the boy them still set up a North American tour.

Everybody's: Are you saying that last year the North American tour was set up without consulting you?

Marley: Yes. Because I tell them don't set up no tour until I tell you. But them don't want to live by that. What them say is 'Bob, it is always good to tour six weeks after your record has been released'. That is fine but suppose my structure don't run in that type of rhythm. I am not going to let them come f..... me up. Is the same reason why I f..... up my toe. If I was in Jamaica and my toe was hurt, I wouldn't work. (Wilson and Herman 1981, 7–8)

By the time the tour reached Madison Square Garden in New York on 19 September 1980 (a day after the concert), Bob Marley collapsed while jogging in Central Park. The next live appearance in Pittsburgh on 23 September would be his last. Print media reporting on Marley's death falls into three general categories: factual, insightful, and distortive. Mainstream media outlets, newspapers in Jamaica, the USA, and Britain contained factual information, as it happened. Some coverage was tokenistic and vague. *The Daily Mirror* reported under the small headline 'Bob Marley in Cancer Riddle' that Marley's 'private Doctor' 'insisted' he was only 'suffering from severe exhaustion' (1980). We can assume an air of secrecy surrounded Marley's condition from the time he collapsed in Central Park, New York, until he went to Germany to undergo unconventional treatment at the Issels Clinic. He stayed there for five months until he was flown back to Jamaica, a trip he did not complete due to stopping off in Miami, where on 11 May 1981, he passed away. Reportage from Jamaica, on the ground, represents the most significant print representation on the singer. It is obvious from much of the data covered in this chapter that he was only featured in Jamaican print when something happened to him, such as the assassination attempt on his life, and his death, which was covered meticulously. In the main, however, outside of *Swing* magazine (which by 1981 had ceased publication) there was no other significant coverage akin to the British or North American music media, who as we have shown, covered Marley's releases and tours in depth, and they also featured in-depth interviews. These kind of media were absent in Jamaica, but beyond the shores of the island they played a significant and more qualitative role with respect to his life and death. Thoughtful obituaries appeared in *NME* (Spencer 1981), *The Guardian* (Williams 2011), and for many of the reports, journalists were assigned to Jamaica to cover the funeral. The live-from-the-scene reports were more in depth, even ethnographic, and television coverage dominated political event that required ample preparation, as Richard Williams said at the time:

> The announcement of the country's national budget was postponed by several days to accommodate Marley's state funeral. Invitations had to be sent out, the mausoleum had to be constructed, and security had to be organised at the National Arena, where the main ceremony would be held. And the prime minister, Edward Seaga, had to prepare his eulogy. (2011)

People lined the streets as the motorcade carrying Bob Marley's coffin made its sixty-mile trek from Kingston, the state capital, to his birthplace,

Nine Mile, in the St Ann's parish. This was the biggest funeral ever held in Jamaica. It was an 'extraordinary carnival of music, prayer and full Rasta pageantry' (Williams 2011).

The death and funeral of the acclaimed singer led to his deification as an extraordinary person who was finally regarded with great respect. Henry Balford, a journalist who covered the event for *The Daily Gleaner* recalls: 'It was the general feeling that the crowd, including myself, Desmond Allen and the late Harris Dias, who covered the event for the *Daily Gleaner*, accepted that we were not only there for the rituals, but also to pay final respects to one of the greatest artistes the world has ever seen' (2021).

The death of Marley also signaled the birth of a legacy. Penny Reel explained this in two lengthy articles in *NME* with the prediction that 'more music will follow' from the early Wailers catalogue and the I Threes, made up of Rita Marley, Marcia Griffiths, and Judy Mowatt, who sang backing vocals for Bob Marley and The Wailers (Reel 1981).

On a similar theme, but with more deified language, Margaret Morris declared in a headline in *The Gleaner*: 'Death of a star, birth of a prophet' (1981). At the funeral, Prime Minister, Edward Seaga gave a eulogy. A day or so after, former Prime Minister, Michael Manley, appeared on BBC television's *Newsnight* describing Marley as 'a most articulate troubadour of the ghetto. He took a folk form and made it part of a universal art' (Denselow 1981).

To conclude on the written press, there is a wealth of information available which we have analysed thematically. Unlike radio and television, print media is where the singer was given the most exposure, particularly in the music press, which was his arena. While this enables the garnering of a lot of information, it is significant to understand press representations vary from ethnographic in depth accounts to inaccurate mainstream tabloid depictions that cast Marley as a kind of 'folk devil' to be feared. The language factor is again a key finding and is fast becoming a key theme of my book as a whole. It is significant however to note that unlike with radio (and as we shall see in the next Verse, television), language was reflected differently with print media. Journalists themselves express views that they could not really understand Marley. Nevertheless, they interviewed him (Murray 1978), while others reflected sarcastically about how some journalists could not cope with Marley's way of speaking (Bangs 2004). At the same time, a couple of journalists themselves actually reflect on it more critically. Neil Spencer argues that many people who interviewed Marley scrutinised his beliefs without really understanding them (1981). This is a very significant idea.

Print media have also provided luminary content on the singer and his views. The interview with Basil Wilson and Herman Hall in the magazine

Everybody's gives a completely different take on the amount of pressure Marley was going through in the last couple of years of his life. During this time, he was also diagnosed with cancer in his toe, which was initially treated. All of this says a lot about a lifestyle and workload that was in one word, simply punishing. Print media, despite popular 'common sense' thinking, as a form of creativity is not the same as 'dancing about architecture'. It has been the most valuable resource available in an archival sense during the course of my research. We learn so much more from these resources, and I also believe there is yet more to learn from material that is yet to be reviewed in a critical academic sense. The same however cannot be said of television, which was, something completely different.

NOTES

1. Although I found some indications of these materials, I could not locate any kind of content online in archived form.

2. Specifically, this will contain landmark events from 1980, such as the Zimbabwe Independence Celebrations in April, the San Siro Show in Italy in June, and Marley's final European concert in Ireland in July. I also plan to draw connections with the One Love Peace Concert in Jamaica, 1977.

3. It is important to note the original articled appeared in *Creem* in the summer of 1976, Vol 8 as a two-part feature by Bangs. Bob Marley was featured on the front cover smoking a joint in the second part of the feature ('Creem – America's Only Rock 'N' Roll Magazine', 2022). I did not have access to the original magazine. The article was found as text in Bordowitz (2004).

4. *Everybody's Magazine* is a Caribbean-American Publication. The interview came out in the June/July edition of 1981 as a fourteen-page dedication. Basil Wilson, also known as Professor Basil 'Bagga' Wilson, was once a football player. He also played for the Brazilian team Santos. Later on, he became an academic. It is interesting that this is one of the most revealing Marley interviews, and it is no coincidence that it was conducted by a Jamaican football legend, who Marley probably looked up to. Herman Hall is the president and publisher of the magazine. He was also present at the interview (*Everybody's*, n.d.).

Verse Five

The Revolution That Was Not Televised

Television, unlike radio, is firstly a visual medium (Frith 2002, 280) and its development had a different kind of relationship with the music industry and commerciality. From the outset, radio had a dependency on music as its main staple diet for content. The music industry's symbiosis with television came later in the 1980s with the arrival of MTV (Frith 2002, 278–79) and in many ways Bob Marley missed out on all of that.

Out of all the media content considered in this book, television underrepresented Bob Marley emphatically, particularly in relation to in depth features and interviews. In comparison to print media, the presence of the artist in person on television, much like radio, is rather sparse, with hindsight. When researching this book, I expected more primary data content given the singer's burgeoning popularity in the decade of his global ascendancy. Television, however, in the 1970s, was a rather exclusive medium to be featured on. In this part of the book we explore the limited television content at length, from different countries, such as the USA, Spain, Canada, and Jamaica, as well as documentaries the artist was featured in that explain, narrate and retell the story of the rising phenomena of reggae and Rastas. There is, nevertheless, a need for an opening reflection that asks a few pertinent questions about why Bob Marley was not featured as often. In other words, why was he omitted just as much, if not more, than the absence/presence of radio explored in Verse Three. Despite the fact that Marley remains a global cultural icon, decades after his death, some may view this glaring omission as peculiar. Perhaps the most glaring example of his absence is from British television. Aside from appearances on programs playing music, Bob Marley never spoke in the first person on television in Britain. This absence is substantial when considering that he was signed to a British music label, Island Records, and that he lived for part of the 1970s in exile in London and toured extensively up and down Britain, which is considered a significant market for promoting music. Some forty years after his death, a reflective documentary called *When Bob Marley Came to Britain* came out (Ramsay 2020). It is questionable why such a documentary took so long to be made. This stark omission is also relevant when considering issues of race and television during this time. These topics were explored at the time in a documentary made for *The Campaign Against Racism in the Media* called 'It Aint Half Racist Mum' (Hall and Steed 1979). Through exposing the obvious and subtle ways racism on television worked in popular and news-based content, they set out to question its impact. Significantly, the program was featured as part of BBC 2's *Open Door* series, and it came with the opening disclaimer that it was made by members of the public using 'their own editorial control' (Hall and Steed 1979). Steed then explained in the introduction that what this disclaimer is effectively 'telling you is that they [the BBC] don't think it's balanced, neutral, or fair [with reference to the program]' (Hall and Steed 1979). The broadcast and the official response in its aftermath demonstrate how regulated and censored television is. The documentary's edited transcript includes the following comments: 'The BBC would subsequently apologise for the broadcast, believing the show to have been "injurious" to the "professional integrity" of such corporation heavyweights as Robin Day and Ludovic Kennedy featured in the programme' ('10. Transcript: It Ain't Half Racist, Mum', 2011).

Reference to the pioneering documentary and its aftermath gives us an idea of the 'whiteness' of British television and how generally through articulating racist and discriminatory content, as a sign of those times, an artist such as Bob Marley never had an 'open door' into the medium in Britain. It can be said of course that The Old Grey Whistle Test (Marley 2014) gave The Wailers a lot of exposure as a band but I am more interested in how the singer spoke in the first person through media. His presence then, despite being featured in British pop charts, was evident only through his absence. As a result, the lack of a narrative presence in interview form is worthy to note as a significant omission in history. Simultaneously, and more surprisingly, we can say a similar thing about television in Jamaica. Marley obviously as featured, however, when he was in the news. This includes the assassination attempt on his life 1976, the One Love Peace Concert in 1978, and the coverage on his death in 1981. There are possibly many reasons for this which can only be speculated on, including perhaps that Bob Marley did not like being interviewed on Jamaican television based on his distrust of local media exploiting his fame. While this is difficult to prove for Jamaican television, we have shown already that he was disappointed with radio interviews being released commercially for profit (Dakodisc 2015; Marley 1991).

What is probably more likely however is that the post-colonial television infrastructure in Jamaica had an aversion for featuring any content with Rastas in it. Rastaphobia can be traced back to atrocities committed against Rastas which took decades to be acknowledged, such as the Coral Gardens Confrontation in April 1963, which is known as 'Bad Friday' to Rastas (Campbell 2014, 200). The clashes between police and Rastas led to the arrest of a hundred and fifty people. Imprisoned Rastas were then forced to cut their dreadlocks (Campbell 2014, 200) – a sanctimonious act of punishment against their belief system. The Prime Minister, Alexander Bustamante, in a discourse reminiscent of the 'wild west' informed the police to 'Bring them in dead or alive' (Campbell 2014, 211). Newspapers, the main media at the time, particularly *The Daily Gleaner* 'whipped up hysteria and demanded that "the Rastafarian problem" described as a problem of the "lunatic fringe", be solved once and for all' (Campbell 2014, 211). It would take an additional fifty years for the Jamaican Public Defenders Office to declare through an official, what happened at Coral Gardens as 'a violation of the human rights of Rastafarians' (UN OHCHR 2017).

The reference to Coral Gardens serves as a backdrop to the lack of media representation of Rastas in the two decades following Jamaican Independence in 1962. Contextually relevant, it goes part of the way to explain why The Wailers, in their original form – Bob Marley, Bunny Wailer, and Peter Tosh – featured on Jamaican television just once with Neville Willoughby around 1967. In conversations with Roger Steffens on this subject I learned that it was filmed in Nine Mile, Marley's place of birth in St. Ann Parish and that 'the tape was erased after it aired because videotapes were very scarce and expensive back then in Jamaica. What a loss' (Steffens 2018a). Marley's other appearances on television in Jamaica, as stated previously, included when he was in the news: namely the assassination attempt, historic concerts, and lastly, in 1980 a live acoustic version of 'Redemption Song' (Marley 1980) filmed at JBC Studios for Dermott Hussey featuring Earl 'Wya' Lindo on guitar. The song would become one of Marley's last recorded video clips and television appearances (Marley 2016; Steffens 2018a).

So if Marley was underrepresented on television in post-colonial Jamaica, and absent completely as an interview guest on Britain, let us look at where he featured in more detail. Seventeen programs included the singer in interviews for my sample. Two of these, *Night Moves* in Australia (1979), and NRK TV in Norway (2011), are more retrospective based content, screened after the singer's death and as such are not considered as solely interviews. The remaining fifteen interview features on television cover the period 1976–1980. During those five years, Marley toured the world. Generally, they can be divided stylistically into two main categories, namely thirteen interview-based programs solely featuring the singer and two documentaries on Rastafarians, one of which included the singer as a significant representative. With such a small sample of content, the value of country demographics quantitatively, in other words, where the programs originated, is not so relevant. Nevertheless, I believe it is important to acknowledge that eight interviews featured in North American television outlets (six in the USA and two in Canada); four in Europe, two in Australia, and one in New Zealand. There may be more content in other countries, but I was not able to locate this based on my extensive searches online.

These fifteen television interviews are based on a question and answer format using conventional over the shoulder filming techniques. Presumably, Bob Marley had little control over the content in terms of question formation and shooting techniques. At the same time, it would be wrong to lump all this content together as there are significant qualitative differences between programs regarding interviewing technique, discursive atmosphere, and formality/informality of content. I want to look firstly at the documentary programs followed by the one interview that I would classify as in a format characterised as 'hard talk' or hostile.

DOCUMENTARIES ON RASTAS – *60 MINUTES*

60 Minutes on the CBS network in USA proclaims to be 'the most successful broadcast in television history' (*60 Minutes* 2022). Beginning in 1968, the show's reporter-centric investigative approach had a different kind of appeal. The program also aired in various countries around the world, including Australia. In 1979–1980, it included two features on Rastafarians: George Negus, a prominent Australian journalist, interviewed Bob Marley on a Trenchtown street as part of a documentary on Rastafarians. I can only speculate that if Marley saw the documentary he would have been dissatisfied and this may in turn have influenced him into not doing a second interview for *60 Minutes* with Dan Rather a short time after. The Negus version of *60 Minutes* is emphatically judgmental from the reporter's opening comments in the studio. Reggae, he claims, has 'become the rallying cry of the not so beautiful Jamaicans, the street people, the dirt poor' and the Rastas are 'strange worshippers of Rastafari, their name for Haile Selassie, the former Emperor of Ethiopia' who are visible through their hair word in 'long pigtails called dreadlocks' (Negus 1979).

The insensitivity of these first remarks clearly show the program's intent to 'enlighten' an audience through a totally uninformed, condescending and colonial discourse. Negus then proceeds to walk through Kingston's ghettos and talk us through, using more patronizing adjectives, stressing 'poverty' and 'degradation' (1979). He speaks on behalf of Jamaicans and Rastas in specific in a way that is condescending and naive. Bob Marley is featured early on, smoking marijuana on camera. Negus quizzes him about breaking the law to which Marley replies 'every law is illegal'. Negus insists 'every law'? Marley explains himself further close up to camera, smoking a spliff, 'Every government upon the face on this earth today is illegal. Not one of them is legal' (Negus 1979). Following this, the camera pans up to a watchtower, a jail guard station, fades out, and eventually fades into barbed wire in the front, where the conversation shifts to discuss the 'gun court', political conflict, and criminality. The camera then returns to Bob Marley, with Negus continuing his naïve line of questioning 'Do you think any of the Rastas have been involved in any of the killings in Jamaica or is that somebody else'? The singer responds, again smoking a spliff, 'Rasta is involved in progress, in making understanding, preaching traditional culture, Rasta a no killers, you have to do good before you can be a Rasta' (Negus 1979). Negus then asks probably the dumbest question of the whole documentary – 'what would I have to do to be a Rastafaree'? mispronouncing the last word (Negus 1979). The next scene, features Colin Campbell, a journalist, talking to Negus by a pool in a hotel. Before this, the reporter lays the ground rules through the narration, stigmatizing Marley in the following way: 'Even if the ganja smoking Marley, ripped out of his head all day, seems hard to take seriously there are Jamaicans like journalist Colin Campbell who don't write him off' (Negus 1979).

Campbell tells Negus that Marley is a leader. Negus tries to reset the agenda by demeaning him as a 'folk hero nevertheless' (1979). The Jamaican journalist realises this comment is a kind of trap so he responds by stressing that Bob Marley is 'probably the greatest contemporary folk hero' (Negus 1979). So even if Negus is being corrected, his effort at framing or demeaning Marley as a 'folk hero smoking pothead' still works as a stereotype because he is the main authority throughout the documentary, even if people being interviewed are not saying exactly what he wants to hear. Seeing this documentary, a number of times, I have often wondered why Bob Marley consented to taking part, given the naivety of the presenter. Roger Steffens offered an interesting explanation. Marley was apparently drawn to doing the interview because of the presenter's surname (Steffens 2018a). Negus in Amharic–a language of Ethiopia – means 'King'. It is not at all clear if Marley had any say in the content of the documentary. Perhaps he chose to sit on the street, smoking herb and talking directly to the camera. I would also assume that based on the experience with Negus that it is highly likely Marley was reluctant to appear in the second documentary by Dan Rather (1980).

Despite its highly condescending and sensationalised approach, the program by Negus appears all over the internet as short soundbite-like snippets, the most famous being the exchange between the reporter and singer on money and riches. 'When you say "rich", what you mean'? the reggae superstar replied with a poker face. Negus asks 'Do you have a lot of possessions? Lots of money in the bank'? 'Possessions make you rich'? Marley fires back skeptically. 'I don't have that type of richness. My richness is life, forever' (Negus 1979). Therein lies the longevity of such documentaries, as online soundbites, never credited to the original source and completely decontextualised in the process. Dan Rather started out on *60 Minutes* as a correspondent in 1968 and went on to become a host between 1975–1981 (The Dolph Briscoe Center 2022). The growth of Rastafari as a movement, the prominence of Jamaican sectarian politics in the late 1970s, and the increasing popularity of reggae and Marley in particular influenced the production of these two documentaries. Surprisingly, Rather's feature on Rastafarians did not specifically include an interview with Marley. He appears on the steps of his home in Hope Road greeting a crowd of people, and Rather makes comments on his success through a sensationalised narrative coupled with filmed images of his uptown home: 'Get the picture, this is the home of the Prime Minister of the country. Just down the road, the residence of the Governor General. And then right here, next in line, is the home of the new prophet of the Rastafarian movement, not a priest, but a pop singer' (Rather 1980).

Generally, Rather's representation of Rastas centers on drugs/ganja, violence/criminality and the threat of 'socialism' (Rather 1980). Even when he makes these accusations to esteemed Jamaican academic Rex Nettleford, who dismissed all of them, the reporter continues by linking the movement to issues of what he terms 'mental health' (Rather 1980). Shifting from Nettleford's University office to ghetto streets, the program ends up at Bellevue, a psychiatric hospital in Kingston, Jamaica. Here the journalist consults Dr. Hickling, who in the reporter's words 'has come to believe that the image of Rastafarians as mad men is rubbish' (Rather 1980). The pathologizing of Rastas as 'insane' and various other distortive representations in the documentary had the effect of a sensationalised reportage aimed solely at a North American television audience. There is however a serious omission in the documentary. Bob Marley is not actually interviewed. We see filmed images of him, in concert, on the doorstep of Hope Road and in the studio making music. There are a number of possible explanations for this. In 2013, Rather himself made a short reflective video clip about the matter, giving lengthy details about negotiations with 'Marley's people' (2013) who agreed to do a short interview on the doorstep of Hope Road. The reporter then proclaims that he never got to meet Marley because he 'collapsed' on the doorstep due to smoking a huge joint (Rather 2013). The colloquial word used by the reporter was that he 'Derek's' on the floor (meaning that he falls flat on his face) – 'before we can do anything and was quickly pulled back in. That's all I saw of him' (Rather 2013). There is however an interesting anomaly here. In the video clip of *60 Minutes,* Rather shares a scene with Bob Marley where he is shaking his hand on the steps of Hope Road, roughly seven minutes into the documentary (Rather 1980). The provenance of his assertion that he never met Marley, which in today's language could well be characterised as 'fake news', leaves much to be desired. It would also be impossible to negotiate all of these shots of Marley without ever talking to him about them. Perhaps a better way of speculating on this is a reluctance on the part of the singer to feature in interview form on *60 Minutes* with Rather, particularly given the stereotypical narratives of his previous experience on the same program (Negus 1979).

Significantly, both documentaries were viewed by millions of people outside Jamaica, many of whom were uninformed about Jamaica, Rastas, and Bob Marley in specific. However, as the first documentaries of their kind, they set a kind of benchmark for the television 'outsiders' looking 'into' what they saw as the 'interesting' and 'bizarre' world of Rastas and Jamaica. One of the key themes articulated in both documentaries relates to criminalization and making Rastas into deviants living on the margins of society. However, nowhere is this more noticeable than in the Canadian television interview Marley conducted with Sandie Rinaldo a couple of years earlier.

HARD NEWS INTERVIEW IN CANADA – SANDIE RINALDO

As Marley toured the world and his popularity increased, he got more airtime on television via interviews. The first interview he did in Canada is probably the most hostile television interview he endured. Sandie Rinaldo is a successful anchor for *CTV News* in Canada. The presenter and journalist has worked at Canada's popular news channel for several decades (CTVNews n.d.). As an up-and-coming television journalist, Rinaldo seized the opportunity to interview Bob Marley backstage in 1978. As a narrative, the program commences on a cliché narrative of an artist and band walking through the streets, getting to the venue, looking around at the hall, and the like. However, the minute the interview starts in a backstage dressing room, the atmosphere switches to a form of journalism that can only be described as 'hard talk' after what appears to be a pleasantly narrated introduction. The opening few minutes are pretty straightforward until the journalist switches from the generic talk on Jamaica and reggae's popularity, to a specific line of questioning on Rastafarians. At this point in the interview, Bob Marley is seated opposite the reporter and appears increasingly pensive, as demonstrated by how quickly his eyes shift in response to the next question. Rinaldo begins a more aggressive line of questioning when she states, 'Rastafarianism is popular in Jamaica, but it has a negative reputation in Canada and the United States. People are involved with drugs, marijuana trafficking, and violence and police harass-. . .' (Rinaldo 1978). At this point Bob Marley interrupts with a biblical reference, with a frown on his face, looking at the reporter straight in the eyes, 'Yeah man, dem crucify Christ, remember, Christ was a Christian and dem crucify Christ saying him is not what him is . . .' (Rinaldo 1978). The reporter then interrupts him saying 'Let's go back to the facts, people have been arrested, the Rastafarians in Toronto for instance, *(Marley in turn interjects "when ah . . .")* have a very bad reputation' (Rinaldo 1978). While the reporter attempts to build a generalization here without any evidence beyond a hyperbolic reference to 'facts', Marley looks up, increasingly frustrated that he has been set up and counteracts in a way that only he could, which ends in a smile 'I wouldn't say that the Rastafarians have a bad reputation – people I would say people give Rastafarians a bad reputation' (Rinaldo 1978). The reporter, understanding this as accusative, increases the stereotype by referring to Marley's look which to 'most people' would be 'strange' and then goes further with the criminalization of marijuana (Rinaldo 1978). At this point, the interview becomes an ideological battleground. Marley halts the barrage of insults with 'Dig this' and makes a reference to the rule of God which is dismissed by the reporter who adds more inflated claims to the stereotypes already presented by saying 'isn't it in fact true that many Jamaicans, people, get involved with the trafficking of marijuana and therefore get the bad reputation associated with Rastafarians'? (Rinaldo 1978). On the last few words, Marley folds his arms, looks up and shakes his head in completed defiance. 'People get trafficking', he says this, slowly, syllable by syllable, confirming that he does not agree with it (Rinaldo 1978). At this point, the reporter senses that it has all been taken to the limit and shifts tactically to focus on his music and his use of words like 'angry' in his songs (Rinaldo 1978). The musical part of the interview, if we can call it that, is very superficial. Rinaldo asks him about how people see him in Jamaica, how wealthy he is, and what he does with his money. Most of these questions amuse Marley and his answers are much shorter than before. The culmination of the interview appears to be so trivialised and ill-informed, with an emphasis on whether people like Marley in Jamaica. Rinaldo ends the interview with what can only be described as a cliché appreciation, 'And if the people are any indication he'll have made it in Canada too. Sandie Rinaldo, for Canada AM' (Rinaldo 1978). Like the previous two documentaries, snippets of this interview can be found all over the internet, emphasizing the hostile segments, or ignoring them. Although in a completely different setting, around the same time as this interview, a group of academics and researchers led by Hall conducted an elaborate study on how British media 'encoded' events so as to help produce a moral panic about mugging in Britain (Hall et al. 1978). Rinaldo attempts a similar thing here with Bob Marley by trying to define Rastas as criminals, drug dealers, and as people, like Marley, who it is claimed look 'strange'. Along with the representations articulated in the two previous *60 Minutes* documentaries, I would argue overall this kind of television content stigmatised Rastas through references to crime, marijuana and judgments on appearance. In the process they reflected a form of 'moral panic' by the makers of television content whereby Rastas became 'folk devils' (Cohen 1972) to audiences who may possibly have only encountered Rastas through the medium of television itself. Out of all the interviews I traced, this one, for reasons beyond my control, also frequently changes web site addresses, with evidence of many dead links online. As a result, it has also been saved online at the web page for this book (Hajimichael 2022). Additionally, it is important to comprehend why this interview was so harsh. Many years later Sandie Rinaldo reflected on it by responding in these terms on the CTV News website:

> 'I wish I could do it again, because there were a lot of questions I asked that I probably shouldn't have at the time', she said of the Marley interview. 'I was told by the news director at the time "be tough on him" because he was advocating a certain type of lifestyle that people should be aware of', Rinaldo recalled. 'I think now, with the wisdom of age, I would have taken a whole different approach because he was an icon. These are lessons you learn as you do your job'. (Commisso 2013)

I find this reflection interesting because it highlights the operational hierarchy within a television news operation where a news director instructs a young woman reporter to be 'tough' on Marley because his lifestyle alarmed 'people' – the audience – and they needed to be alerted about it. The effect of television in this instance was to guide the audience through the use of unsubstantiated stereotypes on Rastas based on impressions created through the medium itself. Television in the three instances reviewed so far 'spoke' about Rastas, particularly in the *60 Minutes* documentaries, without them speaking for themselves. In the Rinaldo interview, we experience something different – an all-out confrontation, hard talk, embattled journalism, where the reporter attempts quite badly to define Marley and Rastas through a moral panic framework. The key thing, however, that links these three texts is a real lack of subjective knowledge on Marley and Rastafari as a belief system and way of life. So clearly, there was no ethnographic turn happening in these texts as television content. I have examined news and documentary television content thus far. Let us now turn our attention to more music-based broadcast content.

BOB MARLEY'S MUSIC TELEVISION INTERVIEWS

One of Marley's earliest television interviews was with TJ Western in 1976 for the television program, *Reggae Music*. The interview aired in Minnesota on a community-based station called KTCA-TV. The station was the first non-commercial public television station in the state founded in 1957. So, this was not by any means a mainstream television station by the mid-1970s, and it remains to this day as a non-for-profit rebranded as TBT – PBS (TVS Wikia n.d.).

The show begins in a studio with two people seated in chairs with a television in front of them. The main commentator, TJ Western, delivers a lengthy introduction to reggae. He also appears somewhat anxious as he swivels slightly in his chair while reading from a script. Afterwards, the opening photo montage set to music illustrates the evolution of reggae. The camera then returns to the interviewer, who introduces Marley and plays the videotape. The camera zooms into the television set and the interview commences (Western 1976). It is not clear if this interview actually aired like this, as there are several jump cuts and at times the audio was not comprehensible enough to transcribe. Nonetheless, the style and format of this first television interview is reflected in the majority of subsequent interviews. Namely, Marley is touring in a particular city, he is then tracked down and typically interviewed backstage in a dressing room, hotel, or studio, with live shots of the singer and band mixed throughout. The other common occurrence is that Marley has a microphone in front of him and the interviewer(s)/reporter(s) is/are there to ask him questions, with the camera frequently focusing mostly on him. There is no real hard talk about journalism as manifested in previous examples. Many of these television interviews that are more music-based are less formal and more laid back. The key thing I found interesting about the Western interview is a reference by Marley to being dissatisfied with how media treated him. This is interesting because it never really came up directly from the singer in data in our previous analysis on radio and the press. The sad thing about this however is that it is not clearly audible to transcribe, and the interview itself is very brief, around two minutes long – although the whole program was fifteen minutes long. However, after the interview, Western makes an interesting reference to what Marley said about media: 'In case you had a hard time understanding what he was saying, he dealt a little bit, with the, er, press, and how they treated him, errm, sometimes they twist things, to mean what they want it to mean rather than what he was, trying to say, or what someone else is trying to say' (Western 1976).

This comment is the most noteworthy portion in the brief interview, as it demonstrates the singer's ambivalence toward the media and press in specific, as early as 1976. But it is such a shame that Bob Marley's actual words on this point in the interview are inaudible.

In 1978, Marley was interviewed for NBC, National Broadcasting Company news, in a second interview by another American popular mainstream radio host, Bruce Morrow. While this is a serious news report, Bruce Morrow, a radio personality, feels at times completely out of his depth. The NBC News interview is primarily based on the fact that Marley was topical and in the news, as a consequence of the tumultuous years 1976–1978, which included the assassination attempt on his life on December 3, 1976, the Smile Jamaica Concert two days later, and the singer's exile in Britain for fourteen months. In 1978, Marley returned to Jamaica and performed at the One Love Peace Concert, in an effort against political sectarianism between the main rival factions (Goldman 1978b).

Morrow focuses on the assassination attempt in 1976, exile in London, and his imminent return to Jamaica. The interview confirms something noticeable from Verse Four: while the printed press mentioned the assassination attempt as an incident that happened, there was very little evidence of trying to find out who tried to kill Marley. A couple of years later, television took on this function more systematically, and as we will see in several interviews, the topic of the assassination attempt would resurface on multiple occasions when Marley participated in television interviews. Morrow attempts to figure out what happened and asks Marley with somewhat jaded questions about if he feels he can 'make it' – in other words survive the concert upon his return to Jamaica (Morrow 1978). At times it is clear from the interview that the question-and-answer format is ineffective, and at some point Marley becomes irritated because he is not being understood. Morrow tries to frame things in terms of gang violence from the start when he says, 'Political gang warfare has plagued the ghetto areas of Kingston for more than a decade now' (1978). Despite asking the singer several times about the assassination towards the end of the interview there is an interesting exchange between the two which demonstrates Marley's sharpness of mind and Morrow's shallowness:

Morrow: Why did they wanna kill you though? Why, why is that? *(interviewer's hand motions to Bob, who is in the frame while he talks. Morrow also raises voice here).*

Marley: Because them don't know, dem figure say, it is a gang ting, which it's not a gang ting. (*The singer is motioning cautiously using his hands. On 'gang* ting' he shakes his head. This part contradicts the introduction as Morrow framed it from the start as a 'gang thing'.)

Morrow: Bob, why are you returning to Jamaica? (Morrow 1978)

The last question feels so odd. Having just spent fourteen months in exile in London and being invited to return to play at the One Love Peace Concert, such a question is superfluous. Marley has a real sharpness in the interview. The fact that he questions the way things have been framed as a 'gang ting' is important to consider. Of course, the interviewer does not see this as critique and the program ends with the hope that the concert is peaceful. In a sense, this follows on from the comment in the Western interview on media, but in this case we can see how Morrow attempts to 'twist' the facts but Marley, very wisely, corrects him.

Several interviews happened in Europe as well, including two in France. These programs are also more like features rather than in-depth interviews. The first was for *Antenne 2*, a public broadcasting channel in France. It is difficult to understand because of the simultaneous translations in French and English (Torres 1977). The other has a feature on Marley's love for football, including lengthy shots of the singer playing the game, but the actual interview is very brief (Blanc Francard 1977).

In Spain, however, a different scenario occurred. Angel Casas and Carlos Tena interviewed Bob Marley in 1978 for Televisión Española – TVE channel in Ibiza. I was fortunate enough when analyzing the interview to have assistance on the translation by an intern student at the University of Nicosia, Anna Millans from Spain. Anna's overall conclusion on this program is worth quoting:

> At the end the two interviewers make fun of some of Bob Marley's answers. They joke about him not being sure about who tried to kill him and about the fact that he knows everything about the Bible by heart. The program ends with them telling despite some of the bad answers (with a hint of condescension), reggae music and Bob Marley are very good. (Millans 2021)

As this is a lengthy feature, it merits a detailed analysis. The interview starts on the tarmac at the airport with Bob Marley and The Wailers arriving in Spain. The sound here is not at all audible due to the jet plane engines being too loud. The group then goes through customs and comes out at the front of the building with the song 'Running Away' playing (Marley 1978a). In the next scene they are in the venue, looking at the stage and the speakers, and Bob Marley plays the congas. The venue is an open-air bull ring, which does feel a bit of a strange place to be doing a concert that speaks about 'peace and love'. The camera then moves to some fields and then to a yellow jeep surrounded by a couple of people (probably the crew doing the interview) and we see some buildings. The music stops abruptly and we go to a close-up of Bob Marley's face and the interview begins. This interview was conducted in an awkward manner. Three journalists – two of whom are men, sit on either side of Marley on the steps, and the third, a woman, is in the foreground. The questions are in Spanish, but Marley answers in English. As a process, this must have taken a substantial amount of time to produce, with some things possibly lost or misunderstood in translation. We are not provided a full picture on this and can only assume the translations for Marley were left out of the final program. After some icebreaker type comments on how good reggae music is and its 'good vibrations', the presenters turn their focus symbolically onto religion and Rasta beliefs, by asking what appears to be a naïve question to Marley: 'Do you think Reggae is a religious music'? (Tena and Casas 1978). Marley's body language as he is answering is interesting. He holds a hand on the side of his head thoughtfully. The journalist translates as he speaks. Marley says 'Reggae music is Reggae music. Reggae music is the King's Music. And ahh, it can be religious . . . can be religious', shaking his head on the second repeated phrase (Tena and Casas 1978). After this, the second journalist quizzes 'And what's your Pope'? – meaning who is your religious leader – followed by a number of questions that link the assassination attempt on the singer's life in 1976 with his alleged 'socialist' party affiliations (Tena and Casas 1978). These links feel awkward and bizarre. Again, we see evidence of focusing on the assassination attempt as an 'unsolved' newsworthy issue. Observing the interview, it is evident that Bob Marley is irritated by the interviewer's repeated attempts to elicit the 'truth' through a restrictive line of questioning. In many interviews with musicians at this point, the strategy would be to change tack when it appears one is losing control. Instead, they continue naively with questions on Haile Selassie which lead to the insulting accusation that, to people in 'Europe' he is an 'authoritarian' 'dictator' (Tena and Casas 1978). Marley responds, shaking his head in surprise 'dictator'? to which one of the journalists confirms 'Haile Selassie was a dictator' (Tena and Casas 1978). With these kinds of closed conclusions to Marley's responses, the same journalist then turns to 'herb', asking 'What kind of erm, importance has hasish or marijuana to the music to get this kind of sleepiness'? (Tena and Casas 1978). By the last word, perhaps he means what is perceived as a 'laid back' 'easy going' stereotypical feeling of reggae. Marley explains the virtues of 'herb' which like anything in moderation, he feels can do no harm. He ends with probably one of his most quoted phrases on marijuana, 'herb is a, is a plant, a tree that grow' (Tena and Casas 1978).[1] The journalists then walk down a path in the next scene talking amongst themselves, joking about some of

Marley's answers, which is disrespectful. The scene then fades to a live event with Marley singing, leaving us to wonder what had occurred. The interview was dominated by the journalists' structured objectives, with little genuine free flowing dialogue. This is followed by live reggae music performed by the singer. What transpired during the interview dissipates – it is forgotten by the time we heard the music. There is a pattern emerging here with various interviews – some questions posed were inconclusive, bad, or intimidating, but they all end with Marley playing music live (Western 1976; Rinaldo 1978; Tena and Casas 1978). Additionally, we can link this to a previous claim by a journalist that people often misunderstood Marley through aggressive lines of questioning his beliefs (Spencer 1981). Well, here we can see this for ourselves and again, I believe, if a group of Spanish speaking students viewed this today, they would probably conclude that it is definitely the wrong way to interview Bob Marley.

1979 was a significant year in Marley's tour schedule for playing in countries for the first time. In April of that year, he performed in Japan, Australia, and New Zealand.[2] I will now move my attention to two of these countries, Australia and New Zealand, where he only performed once as a touring artist. Dylan Taite worked as a television journalist in New Zealand in the early 1970s. The video description on YouTube of his interview informs us that Marley was reluctant to participate (Taite 1979). This is not explained at length in any way, but it could possibly be a sign of the singer's increasing hesitation about doing television interviews, which given some of the material we have reviewed thus far, would seem inevitable. After some persuasion, Taite did the interview and from the start, it is clear he is following the tradition of 'gonzo journalism' (Bingley, Hope-Smith, and Rinzler 2012) with an honest subjective reflection: 'Like many Rastas, Bob Marley talks in a thick Jamaican patois, which at times is difficult to understand' (Taite 1979). I find this thought to be a sincere observation by the journalist himself as an indication of the difficulty he will face understanding Marley. He continues by asking a number of questions reflecting a sense of 'informed naïveté' – such as 'can Reggae be copied'? 'was you always a Reggae musician or had you played rock music before'? and 'How long have you been a Rasta'? (Taite 1979). It is literally as if members of the audience put the questions together. It is quite a clever technique, which Marley, sitting outside in a comfortable chair, on what looks like a sunny day, is content to answer. Taite also combines questions with his own narrated subjective insights. On herb, for example he says:

> Perhaps the most controversial aspect of Rastafarianism is the use of marijuana as a central part of the philosophy officially named Ganja. It's colloquially described by the Rastas as herb, and Bob Marley is said to smoke a pound a week.

It's outlawed in Jamaica, and a convicted smoker can expect an eighteen month jail sentence. (Taite 1979)

Regarding cannabis, the nature of Taite's interview is distinctive. Instead of attempting to frame the subject with loaded questions on criminality (Rinaldo 1978; Negus 1979; Rather 1980). Marley speaks for approximately one-and-a-half minutes freely on the subject and how he sees it, making the interview more ethnographic and significantly more informative. There is also a narrative exchange on media. Again, comments by the interviewer are dubbed in. This exchange is worth considering at length, with Taite narrating: 'Essentially Marley's a quiet man, a difficult man to reach because he's got no interest in the height vibe which preoccupies so many rock stars. He upset many New Zealand journalists by refusing interviews, not because of a sudden whim, but because really, he isn't interested in that type of thing' (Taite 1979).

Taite reveals a lot about Marley here in terms of how he did not like to be in the limelight of the media and how he also refused to do some interviews in New Zealand because he did not see it as something of interest to do. Marley then explains this in the following way:

> Media. . . . *(pauses and thinks)* As if I run a newspaper *(taps his chest)*, I would read a lot of interviews because what I wanted to say, I would get it across. But, when I talk to someone who have to go to someone and then it help to put up their business. And if it too, if it too, militant them try to spread a type of propaganda. I mean, *(for)* me, the media and the media, media is media, *(laughs)* Control! (Taite 1979)

This answer is very significant in understanding Marley's thoughts on media. He explains it elaborately almost as a food chain that props up specific ideas but if something or someone is 'too militant' the response would be to make propaganda about them. Therefore, media works as a tautology; it feeds itself for the purpose of 'control'. The interview ends on a reflection of a 'political type shooting' (a reference to the assassination attempt on Marley's life in 1976) and whether the singer, according to Taite, viewed 'dabbling in politics as a good idea' (1979). There is a noticeable difference here regarding the framing of this subject matter compared to previous interviews. Taite comes across as naïve but he does not try to be intimidating by insisting on finding answers with follow-up questions. Marley dismisses the idea, stressing each syllable philosophically on the first few words: 'Well, you see dabbling in politics, I don't know what that is. It's to stand up and talk for my rights I know what that is' (Taite 1979).

Overall, Taite's interview stands out perhaps in the same way that Lester Bangs' interview does with regard to the music press. Both of them, as advocates of 'gonzo journalism', gave Marley more of a first-person voice but at the same time, expressed their own opinions and subjectiveness without being so directive and intimidating.

The remaining four interviews are North American in origin and flow in a different way. They happened between 1979–1980 with three different people in Black-based media: Gil Noble (USA), Lionel 'Bingie' Barker (Canada), and Earl Chin (USA). Although the interview styles are radically different, these interviews all fit under the category of an emerging trend in North America of Black community-based media, which in the case of two of the interviewers (Barker and Chin) had a strong reggae leaning, although it must be said all three had completely different presentational styles.

Edward Gil Noble (1932–2012) was an African American television reporter and producer at New York City's WABC TV hosting a weekly show called *Like It Is* (IMDb 1990). The program focused on issues relating to African Americans and the African diaspora. Bob Marley was the ideal feature for such a program as many of his songs focused on issues of the African diaspora; his feature on this program is down to earth, ethnographic, and laid back. Possibly one of the lengthiest television interviews he did, at just over twenty-seven minutes, the interview is well informed, and there is a real sense of connection between the presenter and guest. Marley, in his efforts to win over the African American market with his music, probably felt a need to do an interview like this. In the interview, Noble refers to him as 'brother Marley', and they discuss African American realities, African liberation, and Rastafari. There is also an interesting exchange on how reggae evolved from calypso, through to ska and rocksteady, which leads Noble to ask further questions like 'how is ska different from reggae'? and 'how does reggae and ska come out of calypso'? (Noble 1980). These types of ethnographic questions gave room for Marley to improvise and reason, with answers on the tempo and sounds of the music. The interview is conducted in the style of a more polished television program, with an experienced crew and professional editing. Noble is dressed formally in a suit and tie. He appears and sounds like a journalist attempting to learn more about Bob Marley, as he holds a sheet of questions. It certainly is in-depth and brings out a side of Bob Marley which most other interviews failed to achieve. A good example of this is the dialogue that follows on being African:

Noble: Do you think of yourself more as an African than a Jamaican?

Marley: Yeah, because one of the main thing is that we a rasta from we accept Rasta, you become a Ethiopian, which is Africa. Next thing again the history of Jamaica's show the Arawak Indian was living there and it belong to the Arawak Indian. Now, our history show that through slave business? Black people come out a the west and ting you know, so you still figure say Africa is a root, you know, and this is we must return to. (Noble 1980)

As such, Noble is more nuanced and informed. It is an engaging television interview with Marley being the most relaxed I have seen him on camera. The interview also brought out a lot of issues on identity, beliefs, and Marley's upbringing that are absent from numerous other television interviews. Even the manner in which the shooting of 1976 comes up feels random. Noble asks Marley about the meaning of the album title *Survival* and gets a detailed explanation of the shooting, which we have never heard before:

Noble: Did anything happen to you that caused you to write that?

Marley: Well, 1976, dem shoot off a me right. *(Yes)*. And I figured how that a survival. *(right)* I don't know.

Noble: You never saw the gunman?

Marley: I . . . *(pauses)* at that time no.

Noble: But you know who did it?

Marley: Yeah, me know dem

Noble: Were they caught?

Marley: No no bodder caught. The Police just you know, gwaan a ting *(carried on as usual/did nothing)*.

(Camera stays on Marley's face, shaking his head slowly.) (Noble 1980)

I find this exchange fascinating. Much in the same way that Marley opened up about his punishing tour schedule in a magazine interview (Wilson and Hall, 1981) here he is revealing something about the shooting in 1976 which does not appear anywhere else. The common denominator is that he was interviewed by Black media outlets with people of Jamaican origin based in the USA. Essentially Noble is a fine example of a good journalistic practice; ask a good question, and you will more than likely get an interesting answer. But more importantly journalism appears here to be steered in a naturalistic conversational tone. There is no big pre-loaded question on 'gang warfare' (Morrow 1978) or trying to corner Marley politically (Tena and Casas 1978). Noble guides a conversation and Marley speaks freely.

Bingie Barker's interview is radically different. It is conducted in a hotel room before Marley's show in Ottawa in 1979. This interview exists in many formats online, most of which do not even credit Barker, a Rasta, artist, and radio presenter who also worked in the emerging sector of specialist reggae/Black programs through cable television (Barker 2018).[3] His show was called *Sounds Black*. The impression I have from talking to Bingie Barker is he did all this himself with a very small crew and largely as a fan of Bob Marley's music. The interview consequently does not have a very polished feel technically. I assume this is because it was filmed to tape, and then edited for a cable television channel (Barker 2018). As a program it is similar to the previous cable television example we looked at (Western 1976). What is lacking in the quality of sound and visuals however is irrelevant when considering Bingie Barker's enthusiasm and excitement at interviewing Bob Marley. It is obvious from the start, when he introduces Marley in the following way: 'It gives me great pleasure to introduce this man, the man of Reggae, and when you say Reggae you've got to say Bob Marley' (Barker 1979). The layout of this interview is basic. It is set in a natural everyday environment for the singer. Barker sits with a microphone held out to Bob Marley sitting opposite him. He looks excited and anxious about the interview. Marley looks tired physically but he is fully engaged throughout. His tiredness might be due to the fact that this was made in a room (possibly a hotel) after a concert. What is different from previous examples is that here we have two Rastas talking in a manner that this comes across like an exchange on communal issues as an informal dialogue and yet it is so focused. One comment which appears strange and could easily be misconstrued occurs just before the third minute of the interview when Barker makes a plea: 'Bob keep a talking to the people they might never hear your voice again. Keep a talking for a little while until you're cool man' (Hajimichael 2021b). This could be interpreted as the audience possibly not getting another chance to ever hear Bob Marley on Barker's show again, or perhaps Bingie Barker was aware of Bob Marley's health condition, and this comment may have slipped through. Whatever the case, the next comment by Marley, which was his last in the interview, says a lot about reasoning and communication. It gives us a glimpse into his connotative appreciation of a good interview. He is in a way thanking Bingie Barker for giving him the time to say the things he wanted to say. It is also clear that despite how tired and weary he looks, Marley enjoyed doing the interview. Throughout this last comment, and during most of the interview, Barker comments in appreciation (indicated in brackets and italics in the text) in between Marley's words without interrupting him:

> *Marley:* The people have a voice inside of them that talks to them, you know, that is the voice that people must listen to because, in everything you goin' do there's a wrong way and a right way, and if you listen good, you will know the right way *(true)*. You know. Because, there is a voice inside, talking to everyone, seen *(true)*. Seen, So I & I talking is good because reasoning and communication in the world is really the world best, you know, so I want the people to keep on talking to that

voice that is talking to them and deal with the right thing, because everything you going do there's a right and a wrong way *(true)*. (Hajimichael 2021b)

Marley leans back away from the microphone on the last comment, signaling that the interview is done. I quizzed Bingie Barker on the relaxed nature of the interview, despite Marley looking quiet tired. He said the following: 'Bob was very comfortable giving me the interview, and also offered praises to Karl and myself for doing the only black show in Ottawa called *Sounds Black*. I was just as comfy as him' (Barker 2020).

The last two interviews are by Earl Chin. Again, this is a cable television show – and there is an obvious pattern here – the other two shows like this (Western 1976; Barker 1979) also specialised in reggae. Cable television then was the first platform to host reggae television content. It must be said this is a uniquely North American trend, which indicates the music's popularity at the time as a niche music scene. Chin's *Rockers Television* was the first show of its kind dedicated to reggae in New York, USA (Blog Talk Radio 2022). Again, as a Jamaican and a Rasta, Bob communicates with Chin informally, although I would say these interviews are not as well researched and organised as the previous two examples by Gil Noble and Bingie Barker. This first interview was just before Bob Marley's appearance at The Apollo in 1979. It was filmed in a studio (Chin 1979). The second interview was at Essex House, Marley's favourite hotel in New York, where he conducted many interviews with journalists while staying there (Chin 1980). This was Marley's last in-depth television interview before he died. These two interviews find Marley and the presenter in a very relaxed mood conversing about his latest releases and future plans. The second interview features an unplugged performance with Marley on guitar.

The last three examples of Marley interviews represent a different kind of television aimed at reggae/Black/African American audiences. In all of these interviews Marley is far more relaxed. There are no hostile or naïve questions, as we saw with interviews by Rinaldo (1978), Tena and Casas (1978), Morrow (1978), and Negus (1979). One gets a sense from all this that television represented Marley in different ways. Mainstream representations tended to question, critique, and I would even say de-legitimise his beliefs because he was perceived as someone who represented a threat to the establishment. This was done largely through documentaries (Negus 1979; Rather 1980) and hard talk style news approach (Rinaldo 1978). Initially, I expected to discover television interviews from Jamaica and Britain. Surprisingly, I discovered no data for the years 1972–1980. Also, Dylan Taite in his interview with Marley in New Zealand gives a different kind of television representation which gave Marley a voice to speak his mind in a different manner through a 'gonzo journalism' technique. Interesting that Marley could go to the other side of the earth and be interviewed on television but he was not featured at that time, in interview form, in Jamaica and Britain.

Obviously, Marley's death was prominently broadcast on television channels; his funeral was a globally televised event. Many journalists flocked to Jamaica to cover the funeral. While I will not be delving extensively into this topic, I want to draw a look at an important news feature by Robin Denselow for BBC Television by way of conclusion (Denselow 1981).

Marley's burial was unprecedented in Jamaican and international terms, not only from the standpoint of media attention, but also as a historic event mourning the death of a prominent popular music artist. It attracted tremendous attention as a news story and became a significant media moment in 1981.

To begin with, it was Jamaica's first official funeral for a Rastafarian and reggae performer, making it an important day in modern Jamaican history. Journalists from all over the world arrived to cover the event in great detail. Robin Denselow, who at that time specialised as a writer for *The Guardian* on music and politics, was one of them and his television reportage 'live from Kingston, Jamaica' is one of the most important texts on Marley's funeral. In the introduction to the report we are informed 'Marley was the third world's first superstar' – a theme explored at length when we considered press content, and a title the singer himself refuted. Furthermore, the journalist asserts that this was 'the most extraordinary funeral ever given to a pop singer but then Bob Marley was no ordinary pop singer, as Robin Denselow reports from Jamaica' (Denselow 1981). Images of queues of people then appear on screen with Denselow's narrative taking up the claim of how 'thousands paid tribute to the third world's first superstar' (Denselow 1981). In the next scene, the report shifts to what the journalist calls a 'little trouble' with images of tear gas being used to disperse crowds. Following that, he broadcasts live from the scene, with people screaming and tear gas being used (Denselow 1981). Then, the report delves into Bob Marley's career, including how he got his start in the 'ghetto', with views of Trenchtown reminiscent of recent television representations, such as those previously analyzed on *60 Minutes* (Denselow 1981). The next shot, a formal interview with then Prime Minister Edward Seaga, clearly depicts the elitist version of the funeral. I mention this because Denselow had been reporting for five minutes and this is the only Jamaican who had spoken in that timeframe. The next scene, an in-side view of the National Arena Hall, where the ceremony takes place, uses a probing definition: 'the funeral service was a curious mixture of Rasta religious ceremony and pop concert' (Denselow 1981). The elitism of the reportage continues with Prime Minister Seaga's eulogy from the funeral service (Denselow 1981). The news reportage captures a historical occasion but lacks any link with Jamaicans other than those of the elite, and just goes to show that even in his death, television somehow missed something crucial about Bob Marley. This was the only occasion I remember seeing anything about Bob Marley on the BBC during those years – 1972–1981 – which says a lot.

Generally, the singer represented a musical revolution which was only partially covered through limited televised coverage. However, after Bob Marley's death, a new age steadily emerged, and his longevity and popularity as a commodified popstar grew along with his legacy; matters which we will consider next.

NOTES

1. Just like the previous sound-bite comment on 'money and success', the 'herb is a plant' quote can be found all over the internet on social media as an edited video. These clips have become, to coin a populist word, 'mememified'.

2. There is no trace of television or radio appearances in Japan, which seems inevitable given the language differences.

3. It is important to note that during the course of writing this book, the links for this particular video have changed at least five times. Currently, only Part 1 of the interview exists online at the website credited. I did however manage to transcribe all of the interview when it was online. I also interviewed Bingie Barker in 2018. He felt quite bitter about how the video appears online without giving him proper credit. As a result, there are two entries for this video on my citations and bibliography. Part 1 is the first segment of the video, which is just under two minutes long. The other citation refers to my transcription report of the video itself, with the title 'Bingie Barker Marley Interview Transcription Report' credited to Mike Hajimichael (2021b).

Verse Six

Duppy Conqueror – Life after Death

> Yes, mi friend, mi friend
> Them set me free again
> Yes, mi friend, mi friend
> Me deh 'pon street again
> 'Duppy Conqueror' (Marley 1973b)

This song has always struck a chord with me. I am not sure why. Perhaps it is the eeriness of Peter Tosh and Bunny Wailer's background voices which Bob Marley foregrounds with such determination. I also admire the rawness of Lee Perry's production work on the original mix. As a fitting opening to this final chapter, the symbolic notion of a deceased person's spirit remaining 'deh 'pon (on) the street again' seems appropriate. It is essential to comprehend the importance and meaning of the term 'duppy', which can refer to a manifestation of a deceased person's spirit (in human or animal form) or an antagonistic supernatural being (Leach 1961).

'Duppy Conqueror' (Marley 1973b) can take on a variety of meanings depending on how you interpret the phrase, which has linguistic roots in African mythology. A conqueror of duppies can mean someone who fears nothing, not even the dead. As a result, the teenage Wailers became fearless when it came to walking up on stage and singing in front of an audience. The song title has a deeper connotative resonance when seen in the context of Bob Marley beyond 1981, namely that of a person whose spirit will live on forever. All of this can be easily demonstrated, as this chapter explains, in terms of Bob Marley's longevity, legacy, record sales, and global impact as a musical brand. However, some aspects of this impact represent cause for concern. Before elaborating, I would like to clarify that this last part of the book is significantly different in that it does not focus on media content in depth. My main concern here is to chart and discuss the singer's impact beyond his death as a global brand, remixed commodity, and legacy. Without a question, media played a crucial role in this but the key aspects of this process are the singer's deification as a 'legend' and subsequent reification as a commodity. The number of recordings released before and after his death in 1981 is the most significant indicator of this trend. My first step was to conduct a statistical analysis of his releases, concentrating on albums and compilations. This demonstrates how commercially exploited Bob Marley became following his death.[1]

In terms of albums, until 1973, when the band was known as 'The Wailers' or 'The Wailing Wailers', the original group released six albums. After signing to Island Records in 1973, eleven releases followed up until Marley's death in 1981. We may even question *Confrontation* (Marley 1983b). This was the last album to include new songs by Bob Marley. It was released on Island Records in 1983, two years later. The number of albums released after 1981 is much higher, totaling fifty-one representing around 72 percent of all the album releases (Discogs 2022b). The most notable of these, discussed at length in this Verse, namely *Legend (The Best of Bob Marley and The Wailers)* (Marley 1984) has an astounding 429 versions as different editions (Discogs 2022b). The data for compilations is even more astounding. Before 1981 thirteen compilations were released, yet after Bob Marley's death 273 compilation albums came out, with an additional total of thirty-six from unknown sources (Discogs 2022b). In other words, just over 85 percent of all the compilations came out after Marley's death. These numbers demonstrate a form of hyper-exploitation of the singer as a commodified musical product which regrettably often happens when a popular music icon dies. This is summarised in the following way:

> In December 2017, Forbes magazine ranked Bob Marley at number five among its annual macabre list of Top Earning Dead Celebrities, with income amounting to USD 23 million ('Bob Marley's green machine', 2017). Among musicians, only Michael Jackson (USD 75 million) and Elvis Presley (USD 35 million) exceeded Marley's posthumous revenue for that year, reflecting the extent to which his musical empire has become only one component in a marketplace filled with multiple products bearing the artist's likeness and trading on relationships with his songs, such as the Positive Vibration headphones. (Alleyne 2019a, 4)

Simultaneously, despite hyper-exploitation, Marley remains a mixture of many things which pose significant and problematic challenges:

> Marley's militant stardom was a potent mixture. His words of denunciation and comfort have been able to resonate everywhere. Before we can assess the issues

addressed by his art, we must face the fact that his largely posthumous success itself poses profound problems of history, politics and cultural interpretation. (Gilroy 2005, 226)

This leaves us conflicted between a sense of profound admiration for Bob Marley's artistic, cultural, and political achievements as an artist whose sounds and words touched people all over the world and a strong aversion to this vast commercialization, particularly after his death. To understand how the artist got to this challenging dichotomy, some things need to be addressed.

DEIFICATION BY MEDIA

To gain a deeper understanding of these perspectives, we need to explore a number of events and subjects that emerged after Marley's passing. First and foremost, his death, which was not only a subject of national importance for Jamaica, but also for the global media, who observed it closely in previous chapters. With all the press and media coverage that followed Marley's death, his mythical stature began to solidify. The deification of the singer is something I believe he would have opposed, given his humbleness. I would assume Marley would have been dismissive about ideas that he was 'the King of Reggae', 'a prophet' and 'messiah', and various other epithets attributed after his death. Given indications from an interview exchange with Nelson George in 1980 (perhaps one of the last ever interviews given by the artist) there is proof of Marley's reservation toward being dubbed a prophet and this stems from his own religious convictions as a Rastafarian.

Nelson George questions Marley on this in the following way: 'People call you a prophet when you say things like that. . . . Do you accept that term'? Marley replies: 'I am no prophet . . . I just conscious of things that happen. God make them happen. They no happen without him. So I just follow his vision. It is he who give me the inspiration to write. I no do it without him. So what I say comes from him and projects his wishes' (George 2022). The deification of Marley through media paved the way for further commercial exploitation. However, before that could start to happen a number of issues needed resolution.

LEGAL COMPLEXITIES

Marley's death also left many matters, largely legal, in a complicated situation, primarily because he did not have a will, and to twist a phrase from one of his own songs, 'Everything was not going to be alright'. For the next three decades his estate was a contested issue. Based on Jamaican law, when someone dies intestate (without a will), their estate is divided between their spouse and children. Rita Marley, Bob's spouse by marriage had three children with the singer: Cedella, Ziggy, and Stephen. Sharon, a daughter of Rita's by a previous relationship was also adopted by them. Marley also had six other children with different partners, and Rita had another child outside marriage. In total Marley had eleven children claiming part of his estate (DuPont 2022).

Professionally, as an artist, Marley also had people he worked with: The Wailers, in different incarnations, first with Peter Tosh and Bunny Wailer; and then as Bob Marley and The Wailers, post 1974. Many of Marley's songs involved co-writing with the people in these band formations. These all became important players in legal disputes over Marley's song and publishing rights. A third strategic component, perhaps the most important one, was Island Records itself in the form of Chris Blackwell, the founder of the label who played a central and defining role in Marley's transition from a Jamaican to an international popular music icon. This was further complicated in 1989 when Island was sold to Polygram, with Chris Blackwell stating: 'It had gotten too big and too corporate for me and I couldn't really handle it' (Sinclair 2009).[2]

Additionally, of course, in the absence of a will, the Jamaican State itself had a central role to play in the ensuing litigation cases after his death. In fact, courts in Jamaica, the USA, and Britain, would become the battleground for contested ownership of copyrights, fraud, trademark reinforcement, and much more. Eventually in 1991, ten years after his death, The Marley Estate, as ruled by the Jamaican Supreme Court, ruled in favour of Rita Marley, his eleven legally recognised children, and Chris Blackwell's Island Logic Ltd (Caribbean News Network 2016). However, legal battles raged on. Universal Music Group (UMG) for example won a court case against The Marley Estate in 2010 over the rights to many of the Island releases (Stempel 2010). Eventually the legal dispute between UMG and The Marley Estate was settled (Gardner 2012). The legal dimensions of Marley's legacy are multifaceted, continuing even today, with The Marley Estate suing different people all over the world, where Marley's image and sounds are being exploited without proper legal permission. I would like to step back though, to just after his death when one question was on the minds of many reggae fans and Island Records.

WHO IS THE NEXT KING OF REGGAE?

Who is the next 'King of Reggae'? Perhaps an obvious answer would be the remaining and original Wailers, Bunny Wailer and Peter Tosh. During an interview with Peter Tosh, he emphasises that he is about to reform the 'Wailers' as the name belongs to the original members of the group. In the same interview he is also dismissive of comparisons to Marley and attempts to 'brand' himself as 'the leader' and out himself in Bob Marley's 'shoe' (Steffens and Holmes 1983). Bunny Wailer, certainly the most reclusive of the original Wailers trio, had stopped doing live shows in 1975 and would not do any more until nine years later (Bradshaw 1984). However, he never stopped recording and releasing music during this time. His *Tribute* release (Wailer 1982) is one of the finest compliments made to eight of the greatest songs by Bob Marley. He rarely gave interviews and shunned being in the public eye. It is accurate to say 'Unlike Marley, who hardly ever refused an interview, Bunny seemed to prefer to let his music speak for him' (Bradshaw 1984). Despite the honourable and sensitive *Tribute* (Wailer 1982) release shortly after Marley's death, Bunny Wailer would never engage in world tours, mass-marketing, and stepping into Marley's 'shoes'. Comparison was also something he rejected, sometime before:

> People will compare me and Peter and Bob, but that house couldn't be built without the carpenter, couldn't be built without the mason, all those people. All those people have an actual part, you couldn't compare them. One couldn't start, one couldn't work without the other. It would be stupid to start comparing the work the carpenter did with the work the mason did. (Reel 1981)

Of course by the mid-1980s most people had realised there would be no one to replace Bob Marley and the whole pursuit of finding the 'New King of Reggae' was fruitless. A natural progression however did happen. In the longer term, the legacy of Marley would be carried on like an eternal Olympic flame by his offspring. Numbering eleven children, many would walk down the similar creative music and creative path with Ziggy, Damian, Ky-mani, Stephen, Cedella, and Julian leading the way. The organic evolution through time is now into the next generation with Jo Mersa – Stephen's son – and poet/actress Donesha Prendergrast – Sharon's daughter, both grandchildren of Bob Marley. There is no other legacy like this in popular music history that spans across generations in such a manner. There is, however, an element to the legacy that disturbs me and to explore this we need to explore the idea of the re-manufacturing of Marley after his death.

'BUFFALO SOLDIER' UNPACKED

On 11 May 11, 1983, two years after Marley passed away, Island Records released the much anticipated *Confrontation* by Bob Marley and The Wailers (1983b). It felt strange at the time hearing these 'new songs'. We knew 'Redemption Song' (1980) from the release and it had been written and performed live for several years, since the late 1970s. There is no clear indication of how the songs were selected, let alone produced, without Bob Marley's presence. One biographer claims the singer planned this 'as the last part of a trilogy' (White 1983, 332) based on his last three albums which ended with *Confrontation* (1983b). The release was carefully mixed by Chris Blackwell and engineered by Errol Brown with Wailers bass player Aston Barrett (White 1983).

'Buffalo Soldier' (Marley 1983a), the first single released by Island from *Confrontation* (Marley 1983b) was the oddest song on the album and I will explain why it stands out at length. First of all, the song was recorded in 1978, as an adaptation from an original song from King Sporty (Steffens 1996). Thematically, 'Buffalo Soldier' (Marley 1983a) is confusing – inhabiting a space between a partial reading of history with a rebellious militancy. Its main topic is the historical role played by African American soldiers after the American Civil War (1866) in conflicts against indigenous people and tribes in North America (History.com Editors 2018). It is also worth looking into the origins of the song and the etymology of the name itself as many writers have previously glossed over these concerns, giving the idea that the song was composed by Bob Marley and King Sporty (White 1983, 333). While I can accept it is a 'particularly meaningful song' for Native Americans who discovered a 'soul brother' in Bob Marley (Salewicz 2011, 398). I believe the song's meaning and production/creative food-chain are important to consider.

Noel George Williams, also known as King Sporty, originally wrote 'Buffalo Soldier' (Marley 1983a). Bob Marley knew King Sporty from his days at Coxsone Dodd's Studio 1 Records Jamaica (Steffens 1996, 50). King Sporty used to sing the song in his repertoire at Les Jardines nightclub in Miami in the 1970s. Whenever Marley was in town he would visit the nightclub and he told him 'I want to sing that song' (Steffens 1996, 50). The core of this collaboration is that Sporty had a song that Marley liked and wanted to sing. For the majority of music industry professionals, this would be a basic arrangement. Someone composes a song, another person covers it, and cognitively, in terms of copyright, the original composer retains full credit. In an interview with King Sporty for *The Beat,* Steffens, who was also then working at Island Records as National Promotions Manager (1982–1983) 'saw that whole thing go down' when King Sporty was 'bought-out' to not release his original version of 'Buffalo Soldier' (Marley 1983a). In exchange the original writer was given $150,000 but as Sporty explains: 'They didn't give me the money to kill the song. They gave me the money in a deal that we became partners. Instead of me owning the total master it became a joint venture. So it gave them permission that they could even do a version of it' (Steffens 1996, 50).

This was then followed by a litigation case which King Sporty lost (Steffens 1996, 51) and eventually the song was to be co-owned with Bob Marley. While co-writing was a common phenomenon for Marley, 'Buffalo Soldier' (1983a) thematically had a very different resonance. The song delved deeply into the historical context of African American troops in the aftermath of the American Civil War (1886) when the US Congress established six all-Black battalions to 'help rebuild the country after the Civil War and to fight on the Western frontier during the Indian Wars' (Young 2022). The phrase 'buffalo soldier' originated from these indigenous people, who, upon observing the dark skin and curly hair of these soldiers, compared them to the buffalo that freely roamed their plains (Young 2022).

A number of songs had been written previously on the same subject matter and with the same title. There was a funky oral story-telling song by The Flamingos (1970) and a doo-wop version by The Persuasions (1972). It is not clear if King Sporty heard any of these previous songs. Musically they had nothing in common with his own song but in his own words he 'read about it (*The Buffalo Soldiers*) in a book years ago when I was a young man' (Steffens 1996, 50). Therefore, thematically, the song was not an original idea but it became the most known song on the subject matter, and the most successful single to date released by Bob Marley and The Wailers. In Britain the song reached number four and stayed on the singles chart for thirteen weeks (The Official UK Charts 2022). There are also over forty-six different cover versions (secondhandsongs 2022) – and this figure does not include the unofficial ones.

'Buffalo Soldier' (1983a) is also one of Marley's most played songs on radio to date, which is a baffling fact, considering it was released after he died. From a narrative and semiotic perspective, the music video is also important to review. It is notable since it was the first Marley video to feature a narrative plot. It was also the first time I saw Rastafarians acting in a video clip on television. The video itself is a Rasta re-interpolation of the Buffalo Soldier narrative, which, based on my observations, includes well known reggae musicians, such as the members of Aswad, Mikey Campbell (Aswad's producer), and King Sounds, which is edited together with shots in a recording studio with Bob Marley on the mixing desk. These candid shots, filmed some time before Bob Marley died, give a realism of making music foregrounded by a well shot movie with the main narrative of Rasta musicians dressed as Buffalo Soldiers, going about their daily business in a forest somewhere, while presumably fighting a war. In the forest, the characters in the video cook food by their tent, smoke weed, aim and shoot their rifles, jump across a stream, use heavy cannons, and fight in battle. Marley appears in the studio, nodding his head to the music, smiling, almost as if to say 'this is good mix' – which acts subliminally as him affirming the visuals of the video clip. The re-interpolative peak of the video is a Rasta Buffalo Soldier weaving his way carefully and casually through the woods, which are filled with the smoke of war carrying a red, gold, and green flag. The soldiers find their way to a river, where their horses take some water. In the final scene, former lead singer of Aswad, Brinsley Ford, fills his water bottle, looks across the lake, as if to say 'that was a hard day's work'. At no point in the video clip do we see the 'enemy' – the people they are fighting – which makes it quite unrealistic. Perhaps the image of Rastas dressed as Buffalo Soldiers fighting indigenous people would not have worked so well politically. The video was directed by Bruno Tilley, who was the in-house designer at Island Records. This was his directorial debut. He would also later go on to to do the artwork for the *Legend* (Marley 1984) compilation (Tilley 2022).

Thematically, 'Buffalo Soldier' (Marley 1983a) possesses an oxymoronic character. While the song describes how these soldiers were 'taken from Africa' through slavery in order to fight 'upon arrival . . . and for survival', there's no mention whatsoever of the indigenous tribes they fought against. Steffens probed King Sporty on this theme:

> *Steffens*: Let me ask you something about that. Because the Buffalo Soldier, you must have become aware now, killed Indians for white people.
>
> *King Sporty*: That's why the Indians were scared of them, but in the terms, they were trying to get redemption and freedom for themselves, so it's the same struggle. (Steffens 1996, 50)

A final comment on the song relates to its catchiness; namely, that eight-bar similarity with the 'Tra La La' song from *The Banana Splits* television show which appeared on screens in 1968 (Woolery 1985). This uncanny link to a children's television show, however, cannot be solely attributed to Bob Marley. It would also be wrong to assume that Chris Blackwell, the head of Island Records, 'concocted it' after the singer's death in 1981 to make the song commercially successful. The melody was featured in King Sporty's original song. In fact, his mix starts with it as a kind of chant, to get people going. It is not clear if King Sporty was aware of this link with a children's television show; in other words, if it was done deliberately to make the song catchier. However, the *Banana Splits* link does seem odd, even if it happened without King Sporty or Bob Marley knowing about it. The song itself is given a kind of novelty factor through this, which taken into account Marley's seriousness as a songwriter, just feels out of place. Furthermore, taken as a catchy hook, it is probably the most sung part of the song and the thing that stays in our memory in a baited way. This takes us back to Adorno's idea on the popular music that we hear what has already been 'pre-consumed' through 'standardisation'. We already know what to anticipate while listening to popular songs because we have been trained to recognise certain standardised things in music – in this case a melody from *The Banana Splits* television theme – and of course this makes it more 'salable' (Adorno 1976, 27).

A kind of a pattern emerges from 'Buffalo Soldier' (Marley 1983a). I would even call it a template. If Marley could sell more units for the music label after his death with a more poppy, catchier song, despite it elucidating thoughts on a serious historical subject matter, imagine what could happen with remixes, re-issues and compilation albums from the Marley catalogue? This was the first step in the reification and re-branding of Bob Marley as a product beyond his life time in an industrialised sense. The phase of hyper-commercialization would intensify a greatest hits compilation.

LEGEND

Generally, the concept of a 'greatest hits' album feels crass to many avid fans of popular music culture. Many fans see these releases as a way for record labels to cash in on an artist, particularly after they have passed away. The fact that Marley himself did not sanction or agree to such a release through Island Records during his lifetime says something. All of his releases during those years were carefully conceptualised and crafted. To somehow pick the best of this material feels awkward, even weak. Additionally, it feels cruel to repackage music for new platforms and the next generations, because this technique tends to re-contextualise and de-contextualise musical works of art. *Exodus* (Marley 1977a), for example, is so passionately crafted, down to the Amharic fonts designed by Neville Garrick, the long mystical fade-in on the opening track 'Natural Mystic' (Marley 1977b) and Marley's voice just flowing consciousness and love over all the tracks. *Exodus* (Marley 1977a) is a complete work. At the same time, I cannot imagine the gargantuan task Chris Blackwell faced in compiling *Legend* (Marley 1984) but the fact of the matter is, he did not do it. How the release was developed is an interesting case study on meticulous marketing strategies which echoes an Adornian nightmare in terms of baiting audiences, 'hook, line and sinker' (Adorno 1976).

Dave Robinson, co-founder of Stiff Records, an independent British music label, was tasked with assembling the greatest hits compilation (Kornelis 2014). Robinson used a different strategy since he considered Marley had been presented as a 'rebel' and 'militant' of the 'dispossessed' up to that time (Kornelis 2014).

Exodus (Marley 1997a), the best-selling album for the singer, had only sold roughly 650,000 copies in the USA and fewer than 200,000 in Britain (Kornelis 2014). These were solid sales numbers, but Robinson believed that by toning down Marley's militancy, he could be 're-branded' and sold to a more mainstream 'white' suburban audience – 'My vision of Bob from a marketing point of view', Robinson says, 'was to sell him to the white world' (Kornelis 2014). Perhaps this was nothing new; Alleyne claims this process started the minute Marley signed to Island with the release *Catch a Fire* (1973a) when his sound was changed to appeal to a more 'rock'/'white' audience (Alleyne 2000). Blackwell confirms this in a more recent interview. After signing The Wailers he 'advised them [that in order] to get played on radio, they needed to present themselves not as a simple reggae band but as a "Black rock act", and go after "college kids"' (code for a middle-class white audience) (Sisario 2022).

Legend (Marley 1984), however, went one step further through a process of redefining Marley based on a detailed market research plan by Robinson, which even included focus groups. Kornelis explains this in the following way:

> Robinson had a hunch that suburban record buyers were uneasy with Marley's image – that of a perpetually stoned, politically driven iconoclast associated with violence. And so he commissioned a London-based researcher named Gary Trueman to conduct focus groups with white suburban record buyers in England. Trueman also met with traditional Marley fans to ensure the label didn't package the album in a way that would offend his core audience. (Kornelis 2014)

The focus groups concluded that the way Marley was portrayed turned them off. Connotations on marijuana, Rastafari and violence, and even reggae as a genre did not appeal to them. They did, however, enjoy Bob Marley's music (Kornelis 2014). This represents a kind of dubious affiliation with Marley, being turned on and turned off by his music. Their reason was also the image of Marley in their minds, and there was as Trueman says 'almost this sense of guilt that they hadn't got a Bob Marley album' (Kornelis 2014). Many of the respondents had also used the word 'legend' frequently when referring to the singer and this became the main title of the compilation with the additional phrase 'The Best of Bob Marley'.

Robinson then worked on which songs to include. These were played to the focus groups for feedback. The omission of Marley's militant songs, such as 'War' (1976b), 'Zimbabwe' (1979), and 'Crazy Baldhead' (1976a) in favour of more 'love'-based content – such as 'Waiting In Vain' (1977c) and 'Stir It Up' (1975a) is an obvious result of the focus group discussions. 'Get Up Stand Up' (The Wailers 1973) is included, and perhaps it is one of the few 'radical' songs on the compilation along with *Exodus* (1977a). This re-framing of Marley went hand in hand with softening his image. By framing him in a more contemplative manner, the cover of the release tamed the singer's often rebellious visual semiotic. This was all part of a plot to reposition Marely as a more sellable commodity. Robinson outlines this in the passage below: 'If you don't get the demographic right and sorted in your mind, you can present it just slightly off to the left or the right. I thought that was happening and had restricted his possible market. My vision of Bob from a marketing point of view was to sell him to the white world' (Totally 80s 2022).

Legend (Marley 1984) redefined Marley as a marketable commodity, leading to a distortion of who he was. More compilations followed in the 1990s such as *Songs of Freedom* (1992a) and *The Natural Mystic (the Legend Lives on)* (1995). After his death, Marley became a re-defined 'object of consumer desire' as a reflection of 'market driven considerations such as the lucrative cataloguing business of reissuing the work of dead rock stars' (Stephens 1998, 140). The singer became immortalised through *Legend* (Marley 1984) in time as a tautological form of consumer fetishism. The compilation sold twenty-five million copies globally, making it one of the bestselling albums of all time (Schaal 2021). It also stayed in the *Billboard 200 Chart* for over 1,503 weeks which is now even longer than Pink Floyd's *Dark Side of the Moon* (UKMix 2022). The 'new construction' of Marley through *Legend* (1984) resulted in it becoming the mainstream representative of reggae, as Stephens indicates: 'By taking "reggae" and the "revolutionary" out of the conception of the album, Island's producers isolated all the music's meaning into the body of the individual artist himself; hence Marley as the "body of reggae"' (Stephens 1998).

Remixes, box-sets and compilations re-coded and re-framed Marley further in the 2000s. His absence from these processes in the sense of creative production resulted in 'the almost total disassembly of the original recordings, frequently leaving only treated vocal fragments, discards authenticity concerns in favor of commerciality' (Alleyne 2019b, 84). A fine example of this is 'Sun Is Shining' (Remix) which placed the singer over a commercialised house beat template, musically distanced from his roots and completely re-framed to a new generation of music consumers (Bob Marley vs. Funkstar De Luxe 1999).

THE REAL LEGACY

Of course, without being too puritanical, there have been some absolutely incredible versions and interpolations of Bob Marley's songs by numerous artists all over the world after his death. These renditions are also part of his indelible legacy. Let's just take 'Redemption Song' (Marley 1980) which has been interpreted by a vast array of people including Johnny Cash and Joe Strummer (2018), Amazonics (2005), Stevie Wonder (1996), along with some amazing sax solo versions from Dean Fraser (1984) and Courtney Pine (1992). The real legacy though is Marley's offspring; as mentioned earlier in this Verse, the singer's descendants continue to shine. The legacy then is not carefully crafted compilations re-framing Marley, remixing him and continuing to exploit his work; it is in the lineage that grows naturally. Additionally, the Marley legacy relates to how the singer took reggae music to different parts of the world during his lifetime. This contributed greatly to the long term development of a worldwide scene stretching from Norway to Zimbabwe, the USA to Japan, and Australia to Ireland (Concert Archives 2022).

MARLEY REHASHED – DOCUMENTARIES AND THE DIGITAL AGE

I want to comment a little bit on documentaries and the digital age. Although these are two separate topics, I would like to consider them together due to their relative connections. Documentaries about Bob Marley all have two things in common. Firstly, none of them were completed during his lifetime and with his permission. Secondly, they constitute a sort of compost heap in the digital age, with re-edited and regurgitated video and radio segments incorporated as new material and through contemporary social media platforms. For a variety of reasons, the regurgitation is tricky because some of the content was problematic from its origin.

It is difficult to accept the very contorted interviews and contrived discourses from say *60 Minutes* (Negus 1979; Rather 1980) being just juxtaposed and edited into any other documentary afterwards without any kind of critique on its problematic contentiousness. Additionally, some documentary content sensationalises specific interpretations on events that happened, often mythologizing them. The documentary *Who Killed Bob Marley?* (Rare Reels Channel 2011) relies on the 'fake news story' that the CIA was responsible for his death through an intricate process of spiking his athletic shoes with a cancer strain. At the same time, however, one of the most recent examples of the cut and paste type approach, the *Bob Marley: Legacy* series on Netflix, while very well intended, over twelve episodes, sadly regurgitated past video content without any critical perspective (Catarino, McDougald, and Odgers 2020). Hosted by Ziggy Marley, and addressing interesting aspects of Bob

Marley's legacy and contribution to the world, the series could not avoid relying on past footage. I just believe it is a shame that a documentary was not made during the artist's life time and with his approval.

My last point concerns Bob Marley in the digital age, and how these documentary remnants from the past add to a new (based on old content) Bob Marley social media existence. The idea of 'liquid modernity' is valuable here (Bauman 2000) as is the digital utopianism of 'making is connecting' (Gauntlett 2011). These accounts are also completely at odds with each other as Bauman argues we are more consumers than producers in the digital age (Bauman 2007) whilst Gauntlett adopts the position of creativity, connectedness and exchanging ideas (Gauntlett 2011).

So how does Bob Marley fit into these ideas of 'liquid modernity' versus the creativity and connectedness of the digital age? Many of his songs were critical of the dehumanizing character of 1970s capitalism. An example of this is 'Get Up Stand Up', a universal protest anthem that questions the sell-out nature of politics with the line 'you can fool some people sometimes but you can't fool all the people all of the time' (The Wailers 1973). Marley's cynicism towards politics is also evident on 'Revolution' (1974) when he declares that we should govern ourselves and not be fooled by politicians because 'they will always want to control you forever' (Marley 1974). In many ways some of these lyrics would make Marley more of an anarchist and a libertarian than a Marxist revolutionary. These views are best summed up in the following terms 'The cosmopolitan concerns that he articulated from below, in explicit opposition to the destructive, vampire forces of Babylon System, pass unremarked upon' (Gilroy 2005, 226). In this digital age, Marley's 'afterlife' as a commercial commodity, through a vast range of 'liquid' online media resources, have increased his popularity in ways that perhaps he would have questioned because his values and convictions were so solid and grounded. He is one of the most popular posthumous musicians on social media, with the official Bob Marley fan page on Facebook having just under 67,000,000 followers at the time of writing. (Official Bob Marley 2022). A quick Facebook search carried out on 22 August 2022 indicated that there are over forty-two groups on Facebook that use Bob Marley's name – most of which – although this is difficult to estimate – are unofficial and fan generated. By 2013, Marley had the second-largest social media following for a dead artist after Michael Jackson (Gruger 2013). On TikTok, Marley content has over 900,000,000 views (TikTok 2022).[3] Nowhere else online is the idea of a digital media compost heap more evident than on this short-form video hosting site generated largely by users. Clips from interviews, mash-ups created by users, live shows re-edited and songs re-contextualised to frame the lifestyle and choices of users are just some of the vast plethora of clips available. Bob Marley on Instagram – an official account – also has 6,500,000 followers (Instagram 2022). The connectedness of people online to Marley in the age of the virtual and hyper reality is inevitable given his popularity but as Gilroy states, this reflects an ambiguity between fame and dissidence:

> As the posthumous popularity of that music grew, the gravity of Marley's dissidence remained at odds with the commercial vitality of the myths that were intertwined with his uncanny celebrity. In other words, the very same spectral image which made Bob into the global patron of rebels and dissenters, transcended its function as a source of third-world glamour. (Gilroy 2005, 228)

Marley, then, is both a universalised brand and a popular cultural icon with polysemic meanings (Presthold 2020) and a symbol persistently resistant to the pressures of 'Babylon' which 'helps to transmit resources of hope on a different future than the one brought to mind by limitless consumerism and the alienated social relations that he dismissed as a "rat race"' (Gilroy 2005, 228).

While my linkage with Bauman could be considered tenuous in relation to Marley, as a conclusion on the digital age and 'liquid modernity' I want to add a key thought. In 2012, the sociologist was invited to speak at Rototom, one of the biggest reggae festivals in the world (Rototom 2022). What exactly, may we wonder, is an acclaimed sociologist doing appearing at a reggae festival in Spain? The words from a Professor Emeritus at Leeds University echo uncannily like a line from one of Marley's most famous songs: 'We live in an age in which the old paradigms stopped working before the new world was ready', he explains. 'One of the main problems of our time is that we are distancing ourselves from the past at full speed, but without being capable of defining the future'[4] (Seisdedos 2012).

To conclude, Bob Marley's afterlife, in terms of commercial success, is stratospheric. This was largely propelled by the re-distribution and re-framing of his songs through a meticulous process following the release of *Legend* (Marley 1984) and through previously unreleased songs, such as 'Buffalo Soldier' (1983b) and a bit later 'Iron Lion Zion' (1992b). In this very commercialised sense of a greatest hits release like *Legend* (1984), after his death, Marley became something different, a re-positioned rebel who somehow had to be tamed and projected without referring to the word 'reggae' and with a strong emphasis on 'love songs'. At the same time however, the utopian Marley and his phenomenal family legacy in an artistic sense, has the feeling of an eternal flame of resistance passed down from generation to generation, and this is unique in the world and history of popular music. There is no other artist who has left behind such a legacy, and in this regard, Marley is in a league of his own. In this sense he is in no way second to Michael Jackson, or behind Elvis, or on par with Pink Floyd . . . Bob Marley is one of his own, like an eternal flame, which continues to burn, hermeneutically. . . .

NOTES

1. I did this through counting all Bob Marley and The Wailers releases from data online. My focus on albums and compilations was easier to do because although there were numerous singles, many of these were in fact remixes and this made the task of counting them individually much trickier. All the data in this section is taken from the same source (Discogs 2022b).

2. This was further complicated when Polygram later merged with Universal Music Group in 1998.

3. I calculated this at the time of writing this chapter through a TikTok search – it is possible that by the time this book is published, the number might rise to over a billion.

4. These thoughts from Bauman resonate with the lyrics 'We know where we going, we know where we from, We're leaving Babylon, we're going to our father's land' (Marley 1976a).

Verse Seven

Won't You Help Me Sing . . .

Reflecting on this book on Bob Marley and media, the diversity of the content, in terms of format and context, particularly in print media, appears profound. This was not something I expected from the start. Simultaneously, the dichotomy between absence and presence in radio and television content feels problematic, particularly given the limited amount of exposure the singer had on these media in Jamaica and Britain. There is a chronological explanation for the abundance of print content, as the 1970s were the 'golden age' of music magazines and particular brands of music journalism that were more critical, informative, and rebellious (Hoskyns 2003; Jones 2002; Nunes 2004). Simultaneously, this diversity is the inevitable result of Marley constantly touring throughout the world, where given the nature of his everyday musical works, he had to engage with a diverse range of media. This, I feel, is a result of his hard work on the road and the 1970s and the advertising strategies of Island Records. Despite the diversity of content, there are a few obvious differences, usually defined by the orientation of media outlets in terms of audiences and purpose. Mainstream media, in all its forms, and when he was included in it, had a habit of being more aggressive towards Marley. There is a clear fundamental difference between the hard/ confrontational television interview by Sandie Rinaldo (1978) and the more community-based and self-financed cable television interview by Bingie Barker (1979). Contextually, both were conducted in Canada, but they are worlds apart in terms of how Marley was treated and represented on camera. Similar findings exist in mainstream British press coverage where the artist was defined on a tabloid front cover as a 'wild man of pop' (Gibbs 1976). Of course, written completely in his absence, this odd offensive epithet on Marley feels so aggressive. However, he rarely appeared on tabloid front covers.

At the other end of the ecological terrain of print media are the journalists as ethnographers, who were present with Marley at crucial stages of his life to document and give first-person recollections which we explored in depth in Verse Four. Many of the articles we looked at are important historical documents rich in anecdotal and first-hand information, which often give Marley a voice on his own terms. We learned for example, about Marley's play on language and being misunderstood through a surrealistic account of an interview with several American and British journalists in Jamaica (Bangs 2004, 66). Indeed, this recollection made me see the issue of language in many ways. Marley was very conscious at times when people did not understand him and perhaps upped the Jamaican patois to make the journalist's job more difficult. This is a perspective also pointed out in one of the last print interviews with Marley in Britain (Needs 2017). The other side of the coin, and this is one of the major findings of my research, is that language was a much more institutionalised issue in the 1970s in terms of Marley appearing and not appearing on radio and television, through processes of exclusion and inclusion. A lot of evidence was found on this through interview research where we were told the BBC agreed to interviews but never actually played (Tobler 2018) and an anecdotal reference by John Peel where he states clearly that The Wailers (in their original line up) were rejected by the BBC (Marre 2011). Overall, the absence of any television interview with Marley during this period on British television is also a reflection of this exclusionism. It is also perhaps more shocking that there is no in-depth television interview with the artist in Jamaica on the same medium. On reflection, neither of these omissions are surprising given the 'whiteness' of British television (Hall and Steed 1979) the level of Rastaphobia prevalent in Jamaican society in the 1960s and 1970s (Campbell 2014; Grant 2011). Marley's music and legacy contributed to a global shift in perceptions about reggae and Rastafari that extended well beyond his lifetime. If only he could have witnessed these transformations for himself. Despite this legacy, the institutionalised exclusion of reggae by radio and television media goes well beyond Marley as an individual artist. By the late 1990s, reggae singers were covered in depth on one of Jamaica's first music television programs, *OnStage*, presented by Winford Williams (Lowrie-chin 2016). This program gave reggae in Jamaica television exposure, which had been lacking for so many decades. As we have seen, in the USA, specialist reggae television and radio programs began to emerge from the mid-late 1970s mainly on cable and student radio networks. All of this reflects a form of marginalization for reggae in specific during Bob Marley's lifetime. At the same time it feels like too little too late to see more contemporary documentaries on, say, the British Broadcasting Corporation (BBC), which never included Marley when he was alive.[1]

I would also like to reflect on the academic value of research on Bob Marley. As seen in Verse Two, the majority of published works on Bob Marley are biographical in nature, and any new work in this vein often feels like a rehash of what has already been written. Aside from a variety of interesting journal papers, there is a pressing need for more academically rigorous research on the singer in the form of published monographs, and for the establishment of what I dub as an area of research 'Bob Marley studies'. Jacob's idea of Marley being included as part of the Caribbean Intellectual tradition is a significant contribution to this (2015). More research is needed on so many aspects of Bob Marley's legacy, song craft, vernacular style as a songwriter, historic concerts (of which there are many), and Rastafarian beliefs. This book has contributed through a long overdue critical evaluation of media content around on the singer. For many decades a number of video clips (Rinaldo 1978; Negus 1979; Rather 1980) have been viewed but seldom analysed from a critical perspective. In the digital age, people cut these up as snippets and share them without much thought going into where they came from contextually, who made them, and most importantly, how Marley, reggae and Rastas were framed in the process. For students of media studies, there are a number of salient conclusions about the craft of making media about music and musicians that I believe are important. Representation and our part in it is often taken for granted. What are we doing when we interview an artist? Are we examining the dynamics between the interviewer and the interviewee, especially in relation to what we know or do not know about the topic at hand?

My research on media representations about Marley has revealed a variety of content. I am opposed to any grand conspiracy argument that the media consistently misrepresents artists or indeed that representation is a straightforward process of 'them' telling 'us' what to think. I genuinely believe we can learn from seasoned writers such as Lester Bangs, Carl Gayle, Vivien Goldman, John Masouri, Penny Reel, Neil Spencer, and Roger Steffens, to name just a few. All of these writers have a genuine ethnographic sensibility in their Bob Marley writings, in my opinion. At the same time, at the other end of the scale, through a variety of media, but I would say with a heavy concentration on the mainstream, many people tried to demonise Marley and Rastas in general. Sandie Rinaldo's 'hard talk' on Marley on Canadian television felt like a 'hatchet job' (1978). In fact, I show this to my students as an example of how not to interview a singer. The same can also be said of the 'neo-colonial' 'documentary' approach of the *60 Minutes* programs by Negus (1979) and Rather (1980). These distinctions in approaches are significant. They enable us to comprehend how media producers implicitly and explicitly create things through reasoned arguments and production decisions – essentially how they represent. Obviously, these representations are not coincidental; they are intimately related to the intended audience of the respective media texts. For example, an interview in *The New York Times* or a feature in *Playboy,* as representatives of mainstream media, are radically different discursively from interviews in *Everybody's Magazine* aimed at a diasporic readership of Jamaicans residing in the USA. As evidenced by the content itself, these variations are influenced by who frames the questions and how, as well as the intended audience. In some instances, we hear a different Bob Marley, most notably in *Everybody's Magazine* (Wilson and Hall 1981), where Marley comes off as weary and exhausted by life on the road while cancer had taken root in his body. Nonetheless, such material is rarely available unless you have read the magazine, and it can only be located by conducting an exhaustive search of online archives. Furthermore, the magazine did not reach mainstream audiences. It gave a significantly different understanding of Bob Marley and how he was coping with the disease that would ultimately take his life. As such, the diversity of audiences is important in unpacking these nuances and variations from perspectives of research and knowledge. Similar differences exist for television where Marley feels like a different person when featured in mainly American Black media channels (Barker 1979; Noble 1980) which happened later in his career.

Bob Marley's longevity is very commendable as a legacy but problematic in its marketed re-manufacturing sense after his death in 1981. We should never lose sight of what Marley did during his lifetime. There is a lot to learn from all the media content and it was certainly enlightening to consider what Marley thought about media. On this final point, we only see snippets, mainly from television and press interviews, where the artist does not like the way the media 'twist things' (Western 1976) and even considers the media to have a role akin to 'control' (Taite 1979). Clearly Marley conveyed his musical messages with a sense of conviction and purpose and he did not like being misrepresented (Reel 2003). I have often wondered what he would have made of so many releases and products that came out after his death. Would Marley have liked being remixed into a house song? (Bob Marley vs. Funkstar De Luxe 1999). Would the singer have agreed with a deliberately targeted 'greatest hits' album like *Legend?* (Marley 1984). Perhaps we will never know the answers to such questions, but during his lifetime, clearly, the artist was treading a different kind of road and his views as expressed through some of the media content referred to previously, mattered a lot in terms of how he was presented and represented. I will not end this book with a 'Marley is God' type quote (Davis 1983, 270) because I believe he was an exceptionally talented human being who contributed significantly during his lifetime, to changing a world that was so unjust, inhumane, and aggressive. He continues to contribute in so many ways, inspiring people throughout the world. Having reviewed a vast amount of media content about him we can see many different representations of his constitutive existence as an artist, creator, interviewee, revolutionary, intellectual, and as an everyday person whose main mission was simply this: 'One good thing about music, when it hits you, you feel no pain' (Marley 1973c).

NOTE

1. A recent example of this is *When Bob Marley Came to Britain* (Ramsay 2020).

Bibliography

'10. Transcript: It Ain't Half Racist, Mum'. 2011. *Birmingham City Institute of Media and English*. https://www.bcu.ac.uk/media/research/sir-lenny-henry-centre-for-media-diversity/representology-journal/articles/it-aint-half-racist-mum-transcript.

'60 Minutes'. 2022. 60 Minutes Official Web Site. CBS. 2022. https://www.cbs.com/shows/60_minutes/.

Abu-Jamal, Mumia. 1979. 'Bob Marley Interview with Mumia Abu Jamal, Philadelphia, November 1979'. Midnight Raver Reggae and Dub. 1979. https://soundcloud.com/raversecords/bob-marley-interview-with-mumia-abu-jamal-philadelphia-november-1979.

———. 2022. 'Free Mumia'. *Free Mumia*. 2022. http://www.freemumia.com/.

Adelaide, Debra, and Sarah Attfield. 2021. *Creative Writing Practice: Reflections on Form and Process*. Cham: Palgrave Macmillan.

Adorno, Theodor. 1976. *Introduction to the Sociology of Music*. Translated from German by Ashton. E, New York: Seabury Press.

Alleyne, Mike. 2000. 'White Reggae: Cultural Dilution in the Record Industry'. *Popular Music and Society* 24 (1): 15–30. https://doi.org/10.1080/03007760008591758.

———. 2009. 'Globalization and Commercialization of Caribbean Music'. *Popular Music History* 3 (3). https://doi.org/10.1558/pomh.v3i3.247.

———. 2019a. *'Real Situation': The Mainstream Marketing of Bob Marley*. *SAGE Knowledge*. London: Sage Publishing. https://sk.sagepub.com/cases/real-situation-the-mainstream-marketing-of-bob-marley.

———. 2019b. 'Bob Marley: Recorded, Recoded, and Revisited'. *Rock Music Studies*, June 1–6. https://doi.org/10.1080/19401159.2019.1627028.

Amazonics. 2005. *Redemption Song*. Boss N.; Marley CD Compilation. PMB Music.

Annad, N. 2006. 'Charting the Music Business: Magazine and the Development of the Commercial Music Field'. In *The Business of Culture: Strategic Perspectives on Entertainment and Media*, edited by Joseph Lampel, Jamal Shamsie, and Theresa K. Lant. Psychology Press.

Balford, Henry. 2021. 'Bob Marley Laid to Rest'. *Jamaican Observer*. 21 May 2021. https://www.jamaicaobserver.com/entertainment/bob-marley-laid-to-rest/.
Bangs, Lester. 2004. 'Innocents in Babylon'. In *Every Little Thing Gonna Be Alright: The Bob Marley*, edited by Hank Bordowitz. De Capo Press. 2004.
Barker, Bingie. 1979. 'Bob Marley Interview Lionel Bingie Barker Ottawa 1979–11–03'. *Marley Archives YouTube Channel*. https://www.youtube.com/watch?v=EXRdrn_gUfM.
———. 2020. Interview with Bingie Barker by Mike Hajimichael.
Barlow, William. 1999. *Voice Over: The Making of Black Radio*. Philadelphia, PA: Temple University Press.
Bauman, Zygmunt. 2000. *Liquid Modernity*. Cambridge: Malden, Ma: Polity Press.
———. 2007. *Consuming Life*. Cambridge: Polity Press.
Bingley, Will, Anthony Hope-Smith, and Alan Rinzler. 2012. *Gonzo: A Graphic Biography of Hunter S. Thompson*. New York, NY: Abrams Comicarts.
Blanc Francard, Patrice. 1977. 'Bob Marley En Concert à Paris'. Ina. 1977. https://www.ina.fr/ina-eclaire-actu/video/cab7700632301/bob-marley-en-concert-a-paris.
Blog Talk Radio. 2022. 'Rockers Television – over 30 Years of Reggae Music Online Radio by Rockers Reggae'. *BlogTalkRadio*. 2022. https://www.blogtalkradio.com/rockerstelevision.
Bob and Marcia. 1970. *Young Gifted and Black*. LP Young Gifted and Black TR.7909. Trojan.
Bob Marley Concerts. 2021. 'Bob Marley – 1980 01 05 Interview in Gabon Africa'. *www.youtube.com*. 2021. https://www.youtube.com/watch?v=yob3OGrWzjc.
'Bob Marley Official'. 2020. Bob Marley Official. Bob Marley. 2020. https://www.bobmarley.com/.
Bob Marley vs. Funkstar De Luxe. 1999. *Sun Is Shining (Remix)*. Vinyl 12". Edel America Records.
Bowen, Glenn A. 2009. 'Document Analysis as a Qualitative Research Method'. *Qualitative Research Journal* 9 (2): 27–40.
Bordowitz, Hank, and Bob Marley. 2005. *Every Little Thing Gonna Be Alright: The Bob Marley Reader*. Cambridge, MA: Da Capo Press.
Brackett, David. 2008. *Interpreting Popular Music*. Berkeley: University of California Press.
Bradley, Lloyd. 2001a. *Bass Culture: When Reggae Was King*. London: Penguin.
Bradshaw, Paul. 1984. 'Bunny Wailer: The Bright Soul of the Blackheart Man'. Rocks Backpages – *New Musical Express*, 14 January 1984. https://www.rocksbackpages.com/Library/Article/bunny-wailer-the-bright-soul-of-the-blackheart-man.
Brown, John. 1977. 'Queen BBC Radio 1 Interview 1977 Episode 1 (2011 Remaster) (40 Years of Queen Book)'. *www.youtube.com*. 1977. https://www.youtube.com/watch?v=gy2tODOvETA.
Burrell, Ian. 2012. 'DJ David Rodigan Resigns from Kiss FM over "Marginalisation" of Reggae'. *The Independent*. 22 November 2012. https://www.independent.co.uk/arts-entertainment/tv/news/dj-david-rodigan-resigns-from-kiss-fm-over-marginalisation-of-reggae-music-8344087.html.

Bushell, Garry. 2016. *Sounds of Glory. Volume Two, the Punk and Ska Years*. England: New Haven Publishing Ltd. UK.

Campaign to bring Mumia Home. 2022. 'Bring Mumia Home – Stop the Frame Up, Free Mumia Abu-Jamal'. *bringmumiahome.com*. 2022. https://bringmumiahome.com/.

Campbell, Horace. 2014. 'Coral Gardens 1963: The Rastafari and Jamaican Independence'. *Social and Economic Studies* 63 (1): 197–214.

Campbell, Howard. 2020. 'Recalling Johnny Golding's Swing Magazine'. *Jamaica Observer*. 5 May 2020. https://www.jamaicaobserver.com/entertainment/recalling-johnny-goldings-swing-magazine/.

Caribbean News Network. 2016. 'This Day in History: Bob Marley's Estate Is Settled in Court and Left to His Family'. *Caribbean News Network*. 9 December 2016. https://www.caribbeannationalweekly.com/uncategorized/day-history-bob-marleys-estate-settled-court-left-family/.

Carr, Patrick. 1975. 'Bob Marley Is the Jagger of Reggae'. MarleyArkives. *The Village Voice*. 30 June 1975. https://marleyarkives.wordpress.com/2012/09/22/bob-marley-is-the-jagger-of-reggae-village-voice-june-30-1975/.

Cash, Johnny, and Joe Strummer. 2018. *Redemption Song*. 3 X LP Boxset. Joe Strummer 001. Ignition Records.

Catarino, Dezi, Marcus McDougald, and Mark Odgers, dirs. 2020. *Bob Marley: Legacy*. Netflix.

Caufield, Keith. 2012. 'Billboard 200 Chart Moves: Bob Marley's "Legend" Hits 500th Week on Chart'. *Billboard*, 21 December 2012. https://www.billboard.com/pro/bob-marley-legend-500th-week-billboard-200/.

Chat-Bout. 2022. 'The History of IRIE FM'. www.chat-Bout.net. *Chat-bout.net*. 2022. http://www.chat-bout.net/index.php?option=com_content&task=view&id=364&Itemid=149.

Chui, David. 2018. 'The Life and (Uncertain) Times of British Music Publications'. NME. 12 March 2018. https://medium.com/@davidchiu/the-life-and-uncertain-times-of-british-music-publications-8760f5fb0a94.

Chin, Earl. 1979. '(HD) Bob Marley – Interview with Earl Chin (Apollo 1979)'. *Rootsman Jacob YouTube Channel*. https://www.youtube.com/watch?v=iTQd37TBsCQ.

———. 1980. 'Bob Marley – Essex House Interview 1980 – Subtitles HQ'. *Bob Marley Fan YouTube Channel*. 1980. https://www.youtube.com/watch?v=Pi8tIuOmBUo.

Clayson, Alan. 2008. 'Obituary: Mikey Dread'. *The Guardian*. 25 March 2008. https://www.theguardian.com/music/2008/mar/25/obituaries.mainsection?CMP=gu_com.

Cocozza, Paula. 2015. 'Booker Winner Marlon James: "I Was the Nerd, I Wasn't into Sports, Assumed Gay"'. *The Guardian*. 14 October 2015. https://www.theguardian.com/books/2015/oct/14/marlon-james-marley-murder-and-me.

Cohen, Mitchell. 1975. 'Bob Marley et al.: Jamaica'. Rocks Backpages. *Phonograph Record*. October 1975. https://www.rocksbackpages.com/Library/Article/bob-marley-et-al-jamaica.

Cohen, Stanley. 1972. *Folk Devils and Moral Panics: The Creation of the Mods and Rockers*. 3rd ed. London: Routledge, Taylor & Francis Group.

Coleman, Wanda. 1973. 'Wanda Coleman Interviews the Wailers'. *Midnight Raver Soundcloud Channel*. 1973. https://soundcloud.com/raversecords/wanda-coleman-interviews-the-wailers-los-angeles-ca-october-1973.
Commisso, Christina. 2013. 'Sandie Rinaldo Looks Back at 40 Years with CTV News'. *CTVNews*. 6 May 2013. https://www.ctvnews.ca/canada/sandie-rinaldo-looks-back-at-40-years-with-ctv-news-1.1268716.
Concert Archives. 2022. 'Bob Marley and the Wailers Concert & Tour History | *Concert Archives*'. www.concertarchives.org. 2022. https://www.concertarchives.org/bands/bob-marley-and-the-wailers.
Corner, John. 1998. *Studying Media: Problems of Theory and Method*. Edinburgh University Press.
Cox, Chelsey. 2022. 'Fact Check: An Ex-CIA Agent Did Not Confess to Infecting Bob Marley with Fatal Cancer'. *USA TODAY*. 2022. https://eu.usatoday.com/story/news/factcheck/2020/07/27/fact-check-ex-cia-agent-did-not-confess-killing-bob-marley/5461870002/.
'Creem – America's Only Rock 'N' Roll Magazine'. 2022. *Rock NYC*. 11 August 2022. https://rocknyc.live/creem-americas-only-rock-n-roll-magazine-reviewed-issue-by-issue-june-1976-volume-8-number-1.html.
Crenshaw, Kimberle. 2012. *On Intersectionality the Seminal Essays*. New Press.
CTVNews. n.d. 'Sandie Rinaldo'. CTV News. Accessed 15 August 2022. https://www.ctvnews.ca/ctv-national-team/sandie-rinaldo-1.424621.
Cuthbert, Marlene, and Avonie Brown. 1997. 'Local Musicians in Jamaica: A Case Study'. In *Whose Master's Voice?: The Development of Popular Music in Thirteen Cultures.*, edited by Alison J. Ewbank and Fouli T. Papageorgiou. Westport, Connecticut: London: Greenwood Press.
Dalrymple, Henderson. 1976. *Bob Marley: Music, Myth & the Rastas*. Sudbury Wembley, Middlesex, England: Carib-Arawak.
Dakodisc. 2015. 'Bob Marley – the Bob Marley Interviews'. *Discogs*. 2015. https://www.discogs.com/release/6563500-Bob-Marley-The-Bob-Marley-Interviews.
Daniele, Pino, and Antonella Venditti. 2021. 'Bob Marley 40: That Live at San Siro That Changed Italy'. *Rock-It*. 11 May 2021. https://www-rockit-it.translate.goog/articolo/bob-marley-concerto-sansiro-audio-integrale?_x_tr_sl=it&_x_tr_tl=en&_x_tr_hl=en&_x_tr_pto=sc.
Davis, Steve. 1980. 'Bob Marley: an Interview with Steve Davis'. *JahUgliman Vol III*, 1980.
Davis, Stephen. 1983. *Bob Marley*. London: Arthur Barker.
———. 2018. *Hammer of the Gods*. New York: Ballentine Books.
Denselow, Robin. 1981. 'Bob Marley – Robin Denselow: Marley Funeral Report 05/21/81'. *WorldWarXP YouTube Channel*. https://www.youtube.com/watch?v=R-6jghYO8YA.
Di Spurio, Laura. 2017. '"Radiorrhea": An Examination of Mid-Century Youth and Radio Culture in Belgian Pedagogies of Leisure, 1945–1965'. *Paedagogica Historica* 53 (5): 542–60. https://doi.org/10.1080/00309230.2017.1359190.
Discogs. 2010. 'Bob Marley'. https://www.discogs.com/artist/41441-Bob-Marley.

———. 2022a. 'Bob Marley – the Bob Marley Interviews'. *Discogs*. 2022. https://www.discogs.com/release/6563500-Bob-Marley-The-Bob-Marley-Interviews.

———. 2022b. 'Exploring Bob Marley and the Wailers, Compilations, and LPs'. *Discogs*. 19 August 2022. https://www.discogs.com/search/?q=bob+marley+and+the+wailers&type=all&format_exact=Compilation&format_exact=LP.

Dmitry, Baxter. 2017. 'CIA Agent Confesses on Deathbed: "I Killed Bob Marley"'. Web.archive.org. *The People's Voice, Inc. Your News Wire*. 1 December 2017. https://web.archive.org/web/20171201183322/http://yournewswire.com/cia-agent-deathbed-bob-marley/.

Doherty, Thomas. 1984. '*Catch a Fire: The Life of Bob Marley* (Review)'. *Biography* 7 (4): 370–72. https://doi.org/10.1353/bio.2010.0685.

DuPont, Gregory S. 2022. 'ONE LOVE: BOB MARLEY'S LEGACY'. *The Law Offices of DuPont & Blumensteil*. 2022. https://www.dandblaw.com/blog/one-love-bob-marleys-legacy/.

Encyclopedia of Chicago. n.d. 'Playboy Enterprises Inc'. *Encyclopedia of Chicago* www.encyclopedia.chicagohistory.org. Accessed 11 August 2022. http://www.encyclopedia.chicagohistory.org/pages/2816.html#:~:text=Annual%20sales%20of%20Playboy%20grew.

Everett, Kenny. 1976. 'Freddie Mercury on the Kenny Everett Radio Show 1976'. *www.youtube.com*. 1976. https://www.youtube.com/watch?v=mVBs0vquSaM.

'Everybody's'. n.d. Everybody's. Accessed 14 August 2022. https://everybodysmag.com/.

'Exodus – Bob Marley & the Wailers'. 1977. *Top Of The Pops* BBC Television. https://tvrdb.com/totp/?q=Bob+Marley+%26+The+Wailers&r=1&v=1&ob=down.

Finlayson, Angus. 2010. 'The Quietus | Features | a Quietus Interview | the History of Trojan Records: Laurence Cane-Honeysett Interviewed & Mix'. The Quietus. 9 August 2010. https://thequietus.com/articles/04768-the-history-of-trojan-records-laurence-cane-honeysett-interview-young-gifted-and-black-the-story-of-trojan-records.

Fraser, Dean. 1984. *Redemption Song*. LP Pumpin' Air. Island Records.

Frith, Simon. 1976. 'Bob Marley and the Wailers: Rastaman Vibration'. Rocks Backpages. *Street Life*. 15 May 1976. https://www.rocksbackpages.com/Library/Article/bob-marley-and-the-wailers-rastaman-vibration.

Frith, Simon. 2002. 'Look! Hear! The Uneasy Relationship of Music and Television'. *Popular Music* 21 (3): 277–90. https://doi.org/10.1017/s0261143002002180.

Gambaccini, Paul. 2018. Interview with Paul Gambaccini – email Interview by Mike Hajimichael.

Gardner, Eriq. 2012. 'Bob Marley Family Settles Royalty Dispute with Universal Music'. *The Hollywood Reporter*. 7 January 2012. https://www.hollywoodreporter.com/business/business-news/bob-marley-family-royalty-universal-music-279372/.

Gauntlett, David. 2011. *Making Is Connecting*. Polity Press.

Gayle, Carl. 1973. 'The Reggae Underground'. *Black Music Vol 1 Issue 8*, July 1973.

Geertz, Clifford. 1973. *The Interpretation of Cultures*. New York: Basic Books.

George, Nelson. 2022. 'Jah Love with Bob Marley'. *The Nelson George Mixtape*. 2022. https://nelsongeorge.substack.com/p/jah-love-with-bob-marley.

Gibbs, Garth. 1976. 'MISS WORLD GOES into HIDING'. *Daily Mirror*, 17 December 1976.

Gilbert, Steve. 1980. 'Bob Marley Interview Steve Gilbert Part 1'. www.youtube.com. 1980. https://www.youtube.com/watch?v=SHuuXQmc0K4.

Gillet, Charlie. 1973. 'Bob Marley & the Wailers: Catch a Fire (Island)'. Rocks Backpages. *Creem*. May 1973. https://www.rocksbackpages.com/Library/Article/bob-marley—the-wailers-icatch-a-firei-island.

Gilroy, Paul. 2005. 'Could You Be Loved? Bob Marley, Anti-Politics and Universal Sufferation'. *Critical Quarterly* 47 (1–2): 226–45. https://doi.org/10.1111/j.0011-1562.2005.00642.x.

Goldman, Vivien. 1977. 'Bob Marley and the Wailers: Exodus'. *Sounds*. 21 May 1977.

———. 1978a. 'Bob Marley: Kaya (Island)'. Rocks Backpages. *Sounds*. 9 March 1978. https://www.rocksbackpages.com/Library/Article/bob-marley-ikayai-island.

———. 1978b. 'One Love Peace Festival'. Rocks Backpages. *Sounds*. 29 April 1978. https://www.rocksbackpages.com/Library/Article/one-love-peace-festival.

———. 1979. 'Bob Marley in His Own Backyard'. Rocks Backpages. *Sounds*. 11 August 1979. https://www.rocksbackpages.com/Library/Article/bob-marley-in-his-own-backyard.

———. 2006. *The Book of Exodus: The Making and Meaning of Bob Marley and the Wailers' Album of the Century*. New York: Three Rivers Press.

Gopnik, Adam. 2017. 'Hugh Hefner, Playboy, and the American Male'. *New Yorker*. 29 September 2017. https://www.newyorker.com/news/daily-comment/hugh-hefner-playboy-and-the-american-male.

Gordon, Maxine, and Mike Connolly. 2002. 'Reggae the Story of Jamaican Music'. TV Documentary Series. *BBC TV/Palm Pictures*.

Grammy Museum. 2022. 'Marley: A Family Legacy'. *Recording Academy Grammy Museum*. 2022. https://grammymuseum.org/event/marley-a-family-legacy/.

Grant, Colin. 2011. *I & I: The Natural Mystics: Marley, Tosh and Wailer*. London: Vintage Books.

Gruger, William. 2013. 'Bob Marley Rises to New High on Social 50 Chart'. *Billboard*, 2013. https://www.billboard.com/music/music-news/bob-marley-rises-to-new-high-on-social-50-chart-5740510/.

'Gun Court Act'. 1974. Ministry of Justice, Government of Jamaica. 1974. https://moj.gov.jm/laws/gun-court-act.

Hajimichael, Mike 1995. 'Representing Cypriots in Britain (1878–1995) an Analysis of Culture, Representation and Power'. PhD Thesis. CCCS, University of Birmingham. https://www.worldcat.org/title/representing-cypriots-in-britain-1878-1995-an-analysis-of-culture-representation-and-power/oclc/556834844.

———. 2006. 'Revisiting Thomson – the Colonial Eye and Cyprus'. In *Britain in Cyprus Colonialism and Post-Colonialism 1878–2006*, edited by Hubert Faustmann and Nicos Peristianis. Bibliopolis.

———. 2010. 'The Flag on the Hill –: Reflections on Semiotics, Popular Memory Construction and Artistic Resistance through Online Spaces'. In *Proceedings of the*

Art and Social Justice Conference. Vol. 1. Durban, South Africa: Durban University of Technology.

———. 2011. 'Virtual Oasis – Thoughts and Experiences about Online Based Music Production and Collaborative Writing Techniques'. *Journal on the Art of Record Production*, no. 5. https://www.arpjournal.com/asarpwp/virtual-oasis-%e2%80%93-thoughts-and-experiences-about-online-based-music-production-and-collaborative-writing-techniques/.

———. 2015. 'Keravnophone Records: In Pursuit of the Cypriot Groove'. In *Music in Cyprus*, edited by Jim Samson and Nicoletta Demetriou, 175–89. London: Routledge.

———. 2018. 'Bail out – from Now to Never – a Rhetorical Analysis of Two Songs about Economic Crisis'. In *Songs of Social Protest International Perspectives*, edited by Aileen Dillane, Martin J. Power, Eoin Devereux, and Amanda Haynes. London: Roman & Littlefield International.

———. 2021a. 'Social Memes and Depictions of Refugees in the EU: Challenging Irrationality and Misinformation with a Media Literacy Intervention'. In *The Epistemology of Deceit in a Postdigital Era – Dupery by Design*, edited by Alison MacKenzie, Jennifer Rose, and Ibrar Bhatt. Springer. https://link.springer.com/book/10.1007/978-3-030-72154-1.

———. 2021b. 'Bingie Barker Marley Interview Transcription Report'. Unpublished research transcription notes.

———. 2022. 'Bob Marley and Media Research'. *Haji Mike's Web Site*. 10 August 2022. https://hajimike.com/bob-marley-media-research/.

Hall, Stuart. 1997. 'Representation and the Media'. *Media Education Foundation*. https://www.mediaed.org/transcripts/Stuart-Hall-Representation-and-the-Media-Transcript.pdf.

Hall, Stuart, Robert Reiner, Chas Critcher, Tony Jefferson, John Clark, and Brian Roberts. 1978. 'Policing the Crisis: Mugging, the State, and Law and Order'. *The British Journal of Sociology* 29 (4): 511. https://doi.org/10.2307/589668.

Hall, Stuart, and Maggie Steed. 1979. 'It Ain't Half Racist, Mum'. *Open Door BBC 2*. https://www.youtube.com/watch?v=m4oZtBfN87A.

Hearsam, Paula. 2013. 'Music Journalism'. In *Specialist Journalism*, edited by Barry Turner and Richard Orange, 107–23. Oxford: Routledge.

Historic Films Footage Archive. 2020. 'Cedella Booker Marley Interview'. 9 April 2020. https://youtu.be/-kUCbwZtt90.

History.com Editors. 2018. 'Buffalo Soldiers'. *HISTORY*. 21 August 2018. https://www.history.com/topics/westward-expansion/buffalo-soldiers.

Holt, John. 1974. *Help Me Make It through the Night*. 7" Single. Trojan.

Hope, Donna P. 2013. 'GIMME DI WEED: Popular Music Constructions of Jamaican Identity'. *Revista Brasileira Do Caribe* 13, (26). https://periodicoseletronicos.ufma.br/index.php/rbrascaribe/article/view/2078.

Hoskyns, Barney. 2000. 'Bob Marley & the Wailers Interviews, Articles and Reviews from Rock's Backpages'. *Rock's Backpages*. 2000. https://www.rocksbackpages.com/Library/Artist/bob-marley—the-wailers.

———, ed. 2003. *The Sound and the Fury: 40 Years of Classic Rock Journalism – a Rock's Back Pages Reader*. London: Bloomsbury.

Hsu, Hua. 2017. 'Manufacturing Bob Marley'. *The New Yorker*. 17 July 2017. https://www.newyorker.com/magazine/2017/07/24/manufacturing-bob-marley.

IMBd. 1990. 'Like It Is'. IMBd. Accessed 17 August 2022. https://www.imdb.com/title/tt11847040/plotsummary?ref_=tt_ov_pl.

Instagram. 2022. 'Bob Marley – the Official Instagram of the Bob Marley Estate'. *Bobmarley. Instagram*. 22 August 2022. https://www.instagram.com/bobmarley/?hl=en.

Jacobs, Curtis. 2015. 'History as Allegory: Bob Marley and the Rastafarian Perspective of History 1973–1980'. In *International Reggae Conference*. University of West Indies, Mona Campus, Kingston, Jamaica.

Jah Raver, and Fred Reggae Lover P. 2011. 'Midnight Raver'. *Midnight Raver*. 2011. https://marleyarkives.wordpress.com/.

James, Marlon. 2015. *A Brief History of Seven Killings: A Novel*. New York: Riverhead Books, A Member of Penguin Group (USA).

John Peel Wiki. 2022a. 'Bob Marley & the Wailers'. *John Peel Wiki*. 2022. https://peel.fandom.com/wiki/Bob_Marley_%26_The_Wailers.

———. 2022b. 'Top of the Pops (Appearances)'. *John Peel Wiki*. 2022. https://peel.fandom.com/wiki/Top_Of_The_Pops_(Appearances).

Johnson, Richard. 2020. 'The Day Bob Marley Died'. *Jamaica Observer*. 11 May 2020. https://www.jamaicaobserver.com/entertainment/the-day-bob-marley-died/.

Jones, Steve. 2002. *Pop Music and the Press*. Philadelphia: Temple University Press.

Jurgensen, Joe. 2009a. *Bob Marley: The Complete Annotated Bibliography*. Prospect, KY: Haras Publ.

———. 2009b. 'In the Book of Life: The Marley Bibliography'. *The Beat* Vol 28 #1 30–54, 2009.

Kellner, Douglas. 2003. *Media Culture: Cultural Studies, Identity and Politics between the Modern and the Post-Modern*. Routledge.

Kenner, Rob. 2012. 'Danny Sims, Producer Who Signed Bob Marley, Dies at 75'. *The New York Times*, 30 October 2012, sec. Arts. https://www.nytimes.com/2012/10/31/arts/music/danny-sims-producer-of-bob-marley-dies-at-75.html.

Kent, Nick. 1977. 'Bob Marley: Jahve, Mon'. Rocks Backpages. *NME*. 11 June 1977. https://www.rocksbackpages.com/Library/Article/bob-marley-jahve-mon.

Kornelis, Chris. 2014. 'Legend in the Making: How Bob Marley Was Sold to the Suburbs'. *LA Weekly*, 24 June 2014. https://www.laweekly.com/legend-in-the-making-how-bob-marley-was-sold-to-the-suburbs/.

Leach, MacEdward. 1961. 'Jamaican Duppy Lore'. *The Journal of American Folklore* 74 (293): 207. https://doi.org/10.2307/537633.

Learyfan. 2016. 'Today in Counterculture History (12/05) – the Pub – Shroomery Message Board #23895942'. *www.shroomery.org*. 5 December 2016. https://www.shroomery.org/forums/showflat.php/Number/15468091.

Leszkiewicz, Anna. 2020. 'Hermione Lee on How to Write a Life'. *New Statesman*. New Statesman. 21 October 2020.

Livingstone, Sonia. 2005. 'Critical Debates in Internet Studies: Reflections on an Emerging Field'. In *Mass Media and Society*, edited by James Curran and Michael Gurevitch, 9–28. London, UK: Sage.

Longhurst, Brian. 2014. *Popular Music and Society.* John Wiley & Sons.

Lowrie-chin, Jean. 2016. 'Lowrie-Chin Post: Winford Williams – Media Personality of the Year!' *Lowrie-Chin Post.* 3 August 2016. http://lowrie-chin.blogspot.com/2016/08/winford-williams-media-personality-of.html.

Maeder, Jo. 2016. 'How to Interview Bob Marley'. *Vanity Fair*, 11 May 2016. https://www.vanityfair.com/culture/2016/05/bob-marley-interview-death-anniversary.

Malika Lee Whitney, and Dermott Hussey. (1984) 2013. *Bob Marley: Reggae King of the World.* Kingston, Jamaica: Lmh.

Marcus, Griel. 1977. 'Exodus'. *Rolling Stone.* 14 July 1977. https://www.rollingstone.com/music/music-album-reviews/exodus-203046/.

Marley, Bob. 1980. 'Bob Marley – Redemption Song (Live on Jamaica TV, 1980)'. *www.youtube.com.* 1980. https://www.youtube.com/watch?v=EAsWrtgOJJU.

Marley & The Wailers, Bob. 1973a. *Catch a Fire.* LP. Island Records

———. 1973b. *Duppy Conqueror.* African Herbsman LP. Lee Perry/Trojan Records.

———. 1973c. *Trenchtown Rock.* African Herbsman LP. Lee Perry/Trojan Records

———. 1974. *Revolution.* Natty Dread LP. Island Records.

———. 1975a. *Stir It Up.* Catch a Fire LP. Island Records.

———. 1975b. *No Woman No Cry.* Single. Island Records.

———. 1976a. *Crazy Baldhead.* Rastaman Vibration LP. Island Records.

———. 1976b. *War.* Rastaman Vibration LP. Island Records.

———. 1977a. *Exodus.* Exodus LP. Island Records.

———. 1977b. *Natural Mystic.* Exodus LP. Island Records.

———. 1977c. *Waiting in Vain.* Exodus LP. Island Records.

———. 1978a. *Running Away.* Kaya LP. Island Records.

———. 1978b. *Time Will Tell.* Kaya LP. Island Records.

———. 1979. *Zimbabwe.* Survival LP. Island Records.

———. 1980. *Could You Be Loved.* Single. Island Records/Tuff Gong.

———. 1980. *Redemption Song.* Single. Island Records.

———. 1983a. *Buffalo Soldier.* Single. Island Records.

———. 1983b. *Confrontation.* LP. Island Records/Tuff Gong.

———. 1984. *Legend (The Best of Bob Marley and The Wailers).* LP. Island Records

———. 1992a. *Songs of Freedom.* 4 CD Compilation. Island Records/Tuff Gong.

———. 1992b. *Iron Lion Zion.* Single. Island Records/Tuff Gong.

———. 1995. *Natural Mystic (the Legend Lives On).* 4 CD Compilation. Island Records/Tuff Gong.

———. 1991. *Talkin' Blues.* LP. Dermot Hussey. Island Records.

———. *Legend Remixed.* Double LP. Island Records

———. 2014. 'Bob Marley & the Wailers – Stir It up (Live at the Old Grey Whistle, 1973)'. *YouTube.* https://www.youtube.com/watch?v=rf8GjhXvOjU.

———. 2016. 'Bob Marley – Redemption Song (Live on Jamaica TV, 1980)'. *www.youtube.com.* 5 October 2016. https://www.youtube.com/watch?v=EAsWrtgOJJU.

Marley, Cedella Booker, and Winkler, Anthony C. 2015. *Bob Marley, My Son*. Taylor Trade Publishing.

Marley, Rita, and Hettie Jones. 20005. *No Woman No Cry: My Life with Bob Marley*. New York: Hachette Books.

Marre, Jeremey. 2011. *Reggae Britannica*. TV Documentary. BBC 4.

Masouri, John. 2010. *The Story of Bob Marley's Wailers: Wailing Blues*. London: Omnibus.

McAleese, Samantha, and Jennifer Kilty. 2019. 'Stories Matter: Reaffirming the Value of Qualitative Research'. *The Qualitative Report* 24 (4). https://doi.org/10.46743/2160-3715/2019.3713.

McCoy, Quincy. 2002. *No Static: A Guide to Creative Radio Programming*. Backbeat; First Trade Paper Edition.

McDonnell, Evelyn. 2016. 'Do Everything Yourself: The Lessons of Punk Renaissance Woman, Vivien Goldman'. *NPR*. 21 July 2016. https://www.npr.org/sections/therecord/2016/07/21/486885368/do-everything-yourself-the-lessons-of-punk-renaissance-woman-vivien-goldman.

McKnight, Cathy, and John Tobler. 1977. *Bob Marley and the Roots of Reggae*. London: W.H. Allen & Co.

Melody Maker. 1970. 'The Most Popular Paper', *Melody Maker*. 18 July 1970.

Melville, Caspar. 2020. 'On Windrush Day'. *SOAS Blog*. 22 June 2020. https://study.soas.ac.uk/on-windrush-day/.

Michelsen, Morten, and Mads Krogh. 2016. 'Music, Radio and Mediatization'. *Media, Culture & Society* 39 (4): 520–35. https://doi.org/10.1177/0163443716648494.

Midnight Raver. 2011. 'Midnight Raver'. *Midnight Raver*. 2011. https://marleyarkives.wordpress.com.

———. 2012a. 'The Playboy Story plus Live in Minneapolis-St. Paul, 1976'. *Midnight Raver*. 10 April 2012. https://marleyarkives.wordpress.com/2012/04/10/the-playboy-story-plus-live-in-minneapolis-st-paul-1976/.

———. 2012b. 'Bob Marley: Music Myth & the Rasta by Henderson Dalrymple'. Midnight Raver. 3 September 2012. https://marleyarkives.wordpress.com/2012/09/03/bob-marley-music-myth-the-rasta-by-henderson-dalrymple/.

———. 2012c. 'The Shooting of Bob Marley'. Midnight Raver. 31 December 2012. https://marleyarkives.wordpress.com/2012/12/31/the-shooting-of-bob-marley/.

———. 2013. 'Rare Bob Marley Interview & More: Swing Magazine, July/August 1975'. *Midnight Raver*. 1 February 2013. https://marleyarkives.wordpress.com/2013/02/01/rare-bob-marley-interview-more-swing-magazine-julyaugust-1975/.

———. 2014a. 'Dermot Hussey Speaks with Midnight Raver about His 1974 Interview with Bob Marley'. *Midnight Raver*. 2 January 2014. Midnight Raver. https://marleyarkives.wordpress.com/2014/01/02/dermot-hussey-interviews-bob-marley-1974/.

———.2014b. 'Why Marley's Performance at Smile Jamaica Matters'. *Midnight Raver*. 5 December 2014. https://marleyarkives.wordpress.com/2014/12/05/why-marleys-performance-at-smile-jamaica-matters/.

Millans, Anna. 2021. 'Angel Casas and Carlos Tena Bob Marley Interview Translation Report', 2021.

Mlaffs. 2022. 'Mutual Black Network'. *Mutual Black Network*. Wikipedia. 2022.https://en.wikipedia.org/w/index.php?title=Mutual_Black_Network&oldid=1074042175.

Morris, Dennis. 2011. *Bob Marley: A Rebel Life*. London: Plexus.

———. 2022. *Dennis Morris Website*. 2022. http://www.dennismorris.com/.

Morris, Margaret. 1981. 'Death of a Star, Birth of a Prophet'. Digi Jamaica. *The Gleaner*. 27 June 1981. http://digjamaica.com/m/blog/a-look-back-at-bob-marleys-death/.

Morrow, Bruce. 1978. 'Bob Marley Interviewed by Bruce Morrow (NBC News), NYC, March 16, 1978'. *Midnight Raver YouTube Channel*. https://www.youtube.com/watch?v=zstEAjhH0yc.

Moskowitz, David V. 2007a. *Bob Marley: A Biography*. Westport, CT: Greenwood Press.

———. 2007b. *The Words and Music of Bob Marley*. Westport, CT; London: Praeger.

Murray, Charles Shaar. 1978. 'Bob Marley: A Lickle Love An' T'ing'. Rocks Backpages. *New Musical Express*. 18 February 1978.

Needs, Kris. 2017. 'MORE than a POSTER'. Rocks Backpages. *Record Collector*. 17 August 2017. https://recordcollectormag.com/articles/posterhttps://www.rocksbackpages.com/Library/Article/bob-marley-a-lickle-love-an-ting.

Negus, George. 1979. 'Bob Marley on 60 Minutes (Channel Nine: Australia)'. *JAMAUSSIE*. 1979. http://www.jamaussie.com/bob-marley-on-60-minutes-channel-nine-australia/.

Negus, Keith. 1998. 'Cultural Production and the Corporation: Musical Genres and the Strategic Management of Creativity in the US Recording Industry'. *Media, Culture & Society* 20 (3): 359–79. https://doi.org/10.1177/016344398020003002.

Nicholas, Rubin. 2010. 'Signing On: U.S. College Rock Radio and the Popular Music Industry, 1977–1983'. Ph.D. Thesis, University of Virginia.

Noble, Gil. 1980. 'BOB MARLEY – Gil Noble Interview on "Like It Is"'. *DAINE GRANT –Reality and Truth YouTube Channel*. https://www.youtube.com/watch?v=W_rX5iINMrA.

Nunes, Pedro. 2004. 'Popular Music and the Public Sphere: The Case of Portuguese Music Journalism'. PhD Thesis, University of Stirling. https://dspace.stir.ac.uk/handle/1893/24#.YwWvyXZByew.

Official Bob Marley. 2022. 'Bob Marley – Musician/Band'. Bob Marley – Musician/Band. Facebook. 2022. https://www.facebook.com/BobMarley.

Open Culture. 2015. 'David Bowie Becomes a DJ on BBC Radio in 1979; Introduces Listeners to the Velvet Underground, Talking Heads, Blondie & More | Open Culture'. Open Culture. 2015. https://www.openculture.com/2015/07/david-bowie-becomes-a-dj-on-bbc-radio-in-1979.html.

Peel, John. 2010. *The Olivetti Chronicles: Three Decades of Life and Music*. Corgi.

Peterson, Richard A. 1976. 'The Production of Culture'. *American Behavioral Scientist* 19 (6): 669–84. https://doi.org/10.1177/000276427601900601.

Phillips, Chuck. 2002. 'Timothy White, 50; Editor Revolutionized Billboard Magazine'. *Los Angeles Times*, 28 June 2002. https://www.latimes.com/archives/la-xpm-2002-jun-28-me-white28-story.html.

Pine, Courtney. 1992. *Redemption Song*. CD Maxi Single. Island Records.

Playboy. 1976. 'Bob Marley, Prophet of Reggae', *Playboy*, September 1976. 34–35.

Presthold, Jeremy. 2020. 'Between Revolution and the Market: Bob Marley and the Cultural Politics of the Youth Icon Chapter July 2020'. In *Researching Subcultures, Myth and Memory*, edited by Bart van der Steen and Thierry P.F. Verburgh. Palgrave Macmillan.

Prince, and Dan Piepenbring. 2019. *The Beautiful Ones*. New York: Spiegel & Grau, An Imprint of Random House.

Prison Radio. 2021. 'Mumia Abu-Jamal'. Prison Radio. 31 March 2021. https://www.prisonradio.org/correspondent/mumia-abu-jamal/.

Radio Survivor. 2020. 'About College Radio'. Radio Survivor. 2020. https://www.radiosurvivor.com/learn-more/about-college-radio/.

Ramsay, Stuart, dir. 2020. *When Bob Marley Came to Britain*. BBC TV Movie.

Rare Reels Channel. 2011. 'Strange Universe Who Killed Bob Marley?' *Rare Reels Channel YouTube*. 2011. https://www.youtube.com/watch?v=mkpC6exWpUs.

Rasmussen, Kaelin. 2017. 'Stephen Davis'. Boston Athenæum. November 2017. https://www.bostonathenaeum.org/library/book-recommendations/athenaeum-authors/stephen-davis.

Rather, Dan. 1980. 'The Rastafarians – 60 Minutes Documentary'. Ethiopia Forever YouTube Channel. 1980. https://www.youtube.com/watch?v=wkcydVrsHMA&t=30s.

———. 2013. 'Bob Marley Stuns Dan Rather'. *WayWire YouTube Channel*. https://www.youtube.com/watch?v=LkWWII-ntxI.

Reel, Penny. 1981. 'The Words and Works of Bob Marley and the Wailers'. Rocks Backpages. *New Music Express*. 6 June 1981. https://www.rocksbackpages.com/Library/Article/the-words-and-works-of-bob-marley-and-the-wailers.

———. 2003. 'The Night Bob Marley Didn't Play the Bouncing Ball'. Rocks Backpages. May 2003. https://www.rocksbackpages.com/Library/Article/the-night-bob-marley-didnt-play-the-bouncing-ball-.

ReggaeLover, Fred. 2004. 'Voice of the Sufferers'. Voice of the Sufferers. 2004. http://voiceofthesufferers.free.fr.

Ricketts, Ronald, and Mark Dowdney. 1976. 'MISS WORLD'S WILD MAN'. *Daily Mirror*, 20 November 1976.

Riley, Mikel. 2014. 'Bass Culture: An Alternative Sound Track to Britishness'. In *Black Popular Music in Britain since 1945*, edited by Jon Stratton and Nabeel Zuberi, 101–14. Routledge.

Rinaldo, Sandie. 1978. 'Bob Marley Interview Toronto 1978'. Midnight Raver YouTube Channel. 1978. https://www.youtube.com/watch?v=XJD4mnzVY7U.

Robins, Wayne. 1978. 'Bob Marley and the Wailers: Kaya (Island)'. Creem. July 1978.

———. 1981. 'Bob Marley, 36, Reggae Music's Leader, Is Dead'. *The New York Times*, 12 May 1981.

Rockwell, John. 1976. 'Crawdaddy Party Mirrors Magazine'. *The New York Times*, 9 June 1976, sec. Archives. https://www.nytimes.com/1976/06/09/archives/crawdaddy-party-mirrors-magazine.html?sq=springsteen%2520crawdaddy&scp=1&st=cse.

Rodigan, David. 1980. 'David Rodigan Interviews Bob Marley @ Capital Radio – London – (1980) – [1/2]'. www.youtube.com. 1980. https://www.youtube.com/watch?v=a_pgepvJnvg.

———. 2017. *Rodigan: My Life in Reggae*. Constable.

Rodney, Walter. 2019. *The Groundings with My Brothers*. London; New York: Verso.

Rose, Lydia. 2016. 'Foreign Music Dominates Jamaican Airwaves'. Jamaica-Star.com. 14 December 2016. http://jamaica-star.com/article/20161214/foreign-music-dominates-jamaican-airwaves#.WFMGSkSk6FF.facebook.

Rototom. 2022. 'Rototom Sunsplash Europe'. Rototom. 22 August 2022. https://rototomsunsplash.com/.

Rubin, Mike. 2020. 'The Wild Story of Creem, Once "America's Only Rock 'N' Roll Magazine"'. *The New York Times*, 3 August 2020, sec. Arts. https://www.nytimes.com/2020/08/03/arts/music/creem-magazine-documentary.html.

Salewicz, Chris. 1979. 'Bob Marley: A Day out at the Gun Court'. Rocks Backpages. *New Musical Express*. 17 April 1979. https://www.rocksbackpages.com/Library/Article/bob-marley-a-day-out-at-the-gun-court.

———. 2011. *Bob Marley: The Untold Story*. London: Faber and Faber.

'Satisfy My Soul – Bob Marley & the Wailers'. 1978. *Top of the Pops* – BBC TV. https://tvrdb.com/totp/?q=Bob+Marley+%26+The+Wailers&r=1&v=1&ob=down.

Schaal, Eric. 2021. 'Why Bob Marley's "Legend" Sold Infinitely More than Any Other Marley Album'. Showbiz Cheat Sheet. 31 May 2021. https://www.cheatsheet.com/entertainment/bob-marleys-legend-sold-infinitely-more-other-marley-album.html/.

Schruers, Fred. 1978. 'Bob Marley: A Puff Away from Huge'. Rocks Backpages. *Circus*. 6 July 1978. https://www.rocksbackpages.com/Library/Article/bob-marley-a-puff-away-from-huge 1/.

secondhandsongs. 2022. 'VERSIONS Buffalo Soldier Written by Bob Marley, King Sporty'. *Secondhandsongs*. 2022. https://secondhandsongs.com/performance/25233.

Seisdedos, Iker. 2012. 'A Sociologist Takes to the Festival Stage'. *EL PAÍS* English Edition. 21 August 2012. https://english.elpais.com/elpais/2012/08/21/inenglish/1345559081_597442.html.

Shaka, Jah.1982. *The Commandments of Dub 1*. LP. Jah Shaka Music.

Sholle, David. 1995. 'Resisting Disciplines: Repositioning Media Studies in the University'. *Communication Theory* 5 (2): 130–43. https://doi.org/10.1111/j.1468-2885.1995.tb00102.x.

Silverton, Pete. 1978. 'Bob Marley: T'ings Could Be Worse'. Rocks Backpages. *Sounds*. 4 April 1978. https://www.rocksbackpages.com/Library/Article/bob-marley-tings-could-be-worse.

Sinclair, David. 2009. 'A History of Cool'. *The Guardian*. 30 May 2009. https://www.theguardian.com/books/2009/may/30/books-music-island-records.

Sinclair, Ron. 1980. 'Bob Marley – "Mi Dead?" Phone Interview – 1980 Subtitles'. *www.youtube.com*. 1980. https://www.youtube.com/watch?v=KWy2zCJgp7E.

Sisario, Ben. 2008. 'College Radio Maintains Its Mojo'. *The New York Times*, 5 December 2008, sec. Arts. https://www.nytimes.com/2008/12/07/arts/television/07sisa.html.

———. 2022. 'Chris Blackwell Is Music's Quietest "Record Man". His Artists Speak Loudly'. *The New York Times*, 9 June 2022, sec. Arts. https://www.nytimes.com/2022/06/09/arts/music/chris-blackwell-the-islander.html.

Smith, W., Alan. 1984. 'Songs of Freedom: The Music of Bob Marley as Transformative Education'. 1984. https://citeseerx.ist.psu.edu/viewdoc/summary?doi=10.1.1.531.3729.

Spencer, Neil. 1981. 'A Man for All Reasoning'. Midnight Raver. *New Musical Express*, 12 May 1981. https://marleyarkives.wordpress.com/tag/catch-a-fire/.

Stand, Mike. 1980. 'Bob Marley: Better off Dread'. Rocks Backpages. *Smash Hits*. 7 August 1980. https://www.rocksbackpages.com/Library/Article/bob-marley-better-off-dread.

Steffens, Roger. 1996. 'KING SPORTY: Buffalo Soldier: the National Anthem of Black People'. *The Beat* Vol 15 #3, 1996.

———. 2018a. Interview with Roger Steffens – Skype Interview by Mike Hajimichael.

———. 2018b. *So Much Things to Say: The Oral History of Bob Marley*. New York, NY: W.W. Norton & Company.

Steffens, Roger, and Hank Holmes. 1983. 'Peter Tosh Interviewed by Roger Steffens & Hank Holmes, Hollywood, 1983'. *JAH RAVER YouTube Channel*. https://www.youtube.com/watch?v=FYIkI4j3T7M.

Stempel, Jonathan. 2010. 'Bob Marley Family Loses Case over Hit Records'. *Reuters*, 13 September 2010. https://www.reuters.com/article/bobmarley-ruling-idUSN1318377120100913.

Stephens, Michelle A. 1998. 'Babylon's "Natural Mystic": The North American Music Industry, The Legend of Bob Marley, and the Incorporation of Transnationalism'. *Cultural Studies* 12 (2): 139–67. https://doi.org/10.1080/095023898335519.

Strausser, Jay. 1980. 'Bob Marley – Last Phone Interview November 1980 – Subtitles'. *www.youtube.com*. 1980. https://www.youtube.com/watch?v=DGO7kxkQGHk.

Streeter, Thomas. 1995. 'No Respect? Disciplinarity and Media Studies in Communication'. *Communication Theory* 5 (2): 117–29.

Swenson, John. 1977. 'Marley Beats the Devil'. Rocks Backpages. *Rolling Stone*. 12 November 1977. https://www.rocksbackpages.com/Library/Article/marley-beats-the-devil.

Taite, Dylan. 1979. 'Bob Marley – 1979 Interview in New Zealand'. *RVP Group*. https://www.youtube.com/watch?v=xiaZJdOqHw0.

Tapalaga, Andrei. 2022. 'Why Did the CIA Try to Kill Bob Marley?' *Medium*. 4 April 2022. https://historyofyesterday.com/why-did-the-cia-try-to-kill-bob-marley-29cfb78ca894.

Taylor, Don, and Mike Henry. 2003. *Marley and Me: The Real Bob Marley Story*. New York: Barricade; Hadleigh.

Taylor, Timothy D. 2002. 'Music and the Rise of Radio in 1920s America: Technological Imperialism, Socialization, and the Transformation of Intimacy'. *Historical Journal of Film, Radio and Television* 22 (4): 425–43. https://doi.org/10.1080/0143968022000012138.

Tenna, Carlos, and Angel Casas. 1978. 'Bob Marley Interview Spain 1978'. *Reggaeman91 YouTube Channel*. 1978. https://www.youtube.com/watch?v=nXL1C16MVx0.

Terrell, Tom. 2004. 'The Rasta Prophet of Reggae Music Speaks'. In *Every Little Thing Gonna Be Alright: The Bob Marley*, edited by Hank Bordowitz. De Capo Press. 2004.

The Bob Marley Foundation. 2022. 'Marley for Education'. *The Bob Marley Foundation*. 2022. https://bobmarleyfoundation.org/marley-for-education/.

The Daily Gleaner. 1976. 'Reggae – Musical Tidal Wave . . . Bob Marley the "Prophet"'. *The Daily Gleaner*, 7 September 1976.

The Daily Mirror. 1980. 'Bob Marley in Cancer Riddle', *The Daily Mirror*. 13 October 1980.

The Dolph Briscoe Center. 2022. '60 Minutes | Dan Rather'. *Danratherjournalist.org*. 2022. https://danratherjournalist.org/investigative-journalist/60-minutes.

The Flamingos. 1970. *Buffalo Soldier*. Single. Polydor. *Discogs*. https://www.discogs.com/master/563713-Flamingos-Buffalo-Soldier.

The Official UK Charts. 2022. 'Official Singles Chart Results Matching: Buffalo Soldier'. *Official Charts*. 2022. https://www.officialcharts.com/search/singles/buffalo-soldier/.

The Persuasions. 1972. *Buffalo Soldier*. Single. Capitol Records. *Discogs*. https://www.discogs.com/release/2880664-The-Persuasions-Buffalo-Soldier.

The Piglets. 1971. *Johnny Reggae*. 7" Single. Bell Records. 2008, 007.

The Wailers. 1973. *Get up Stand Up*. 7" Single. Island Records.

TikTok. 2022. 'Discover Bob Marley's Popular Videos'. *TikTok*. 22 August 2022. https://www.tiktok.com/discover/Bob-Marley?lang=en.

Tilley, Bruno. 2022. 'Bruno Tilley Creative Consultant'. *Bruno Tilley*. 2022. https://www.brunotilley.com/reggae.

Tobler, John. 2018. Interview with John Tobler – email Interview by Mike Hajimichael.

tolsen. 2013. 'Billboard Hot 100'. *Billboard*. 2 January 2013. https://www.billboard.com/charts/hot-100/1968-07-20/.

Top Gear. 1973. '1973-11-26 BBC Bob Marley Interview, London'. *Soundcloud.com*. 1973. https://soundcloud.com/jahraverseh/1973-11-26-bbc-interview#t=0:00.

Torres, Dominique. 1977. 'Interview'. *Voice of the Sufferers*. 1977. http://voiceofthesufferers.free.fr/interview_1977_dominique_torres.html.

Totally 80s. 2022. 'May 1984: Bob Marley and The Wailers' "Legend" Album Released'. *Totally 80s*. 2022. https://totally80s.com/article/may-1984-bob-marley-and-wailers-legend-album-released.

Toynbee, Jason. 1993. 'Policing Bohemia, Pinning up Grunge: The Music Press and Generic Change in British Pop and Rock'. *Popular Music* 12 (3): 289–300. https://doi.org/10.1017/s0261143000005730.

———. 2007. *Herald of a Postcolonial World?* Oxford: Polity Press.

TVS Wikia. n.d. 'KTCA'. *TVS Wikia*. Accessed 15 August 2022. https://tvstations.fandom.com/wiki/KTCA.

UKMix. 2022. 'Billboard Bulletin'. *UKMix*. 2022. https://www.ukmix.org/forum/chart-discussion/chart-analysis/10829596-us-billboard-charts-26-02-2022/page6.

Umberger, Daryl. n.d. 'Rolling Stone'. *St. James Encyclopedia of Popular Culture*. Accessed 22 August 2022. https://www.encyclopedia.com/media/encyclopedias-almanacs-transcripts-and-maps/rolling-stone.

UN OHCHR. 2017. 'After More than Half a Century, a Community Receives Justice'. United Nations Office of the High Commissioner. 26 May 2017. https://www.ohchr.org/en/stories/2017/05/after-more-half-century-community-receives-justice.

Unterberger, Richie. 2017. *Bob Marley and the Wailers: The Ultimate Illustrated History*. Voyageur Press.

Voice of The Sufferers. 2018. '1973 – Bob Marley and the Wailers – Catch a Fire Press Kit – Island Records'. *Voiceofthesufferers.free.fr*. 2018. http://voiceofthesufferers.free.fr/promo_press_kit_catch_a_fire_1973.html.

Wailer, Bunny. 1982. *Tribute*. LP. Solomonic.

Wallace, Leonie. 2009. 'Bob Marley: The Ideal Teaching Tool'. *Academia.edu*. 2009. https://www.academia.edu/7579696/WALLACE_BOB_MARLEY_THE_IDEAL_TEACHING_TOOL

Western, TJ. 1976. 'Bob Marley Interview'. *TJ Western YouTube Channel*. https://www.youtube.com/watch?v=RbZnuBD8sBc.

White, Timothy. 1983. *Catch a Fire: The Life of Bob Marley*. New York: University of Hawaii Press.

Wikipedia. 2022. 'Uprising Tour'. *Wikipedia*. 2022. https://en.wikipedia.org/w/index.php?title=Uprising_Tour&oldid=1072900020.

Wiley, Christopher, and Paul Watt. 2019. 'Musical Biography in the Musicological Arena'. *Journal of Musicological Research* 38 (3–4): 187–92. https://doi.org/10.1080/01411896.2019.1644140.

Williams, Paul. 2002. *The Crawdaddy! Book: Writings (and Images) from the Magazine of Rock*. Milwaukee, WI: Hal Leonard.

Williams, Richard. 1972. 'Reggae: Black Gold of Jamaica'. Rocks Backpages. *Melody Maker*. 30 September 1972. https://www.rocksbackpages.com/Library/Article/reggae-black-gold-of-jamaica.

———. 1973. 'Bob Marley: The First Genius of Reggae'. Rocks Backpages. *Melody Maker*. 22 April 1973. https://www.rocksbackpages.com/Library/Article/bob-marley-the-first-genius-of-reggae.

———. 2011. 'Bob Marley's Funeral, 21 May 1981: A Day of Jamaican History'. *The Guardian*. 24 April 2011. https://www.theguardian.com/music/2011/apr/24/bob-marley-funeral-richard-williams.

Willis, Barry. 2002. 'Timothy White, 1952–2002'. *Stereophile.com*. 30 June 2002. https://www.stereophile.com/news/11378/index.html.

Willoughby, Neville. 1980. 'Bob Marley – the Bob Marley Interviews'. *Discogs*. 1980. https://www.discogs.com/release/6563500-Bob-Marley-The-Bob-Marley-Interviews.

Wilson, Basil, and Hall, Herman. 1981. 'Marley in His Own Words'. *Everybody's Magazine*, 1981. 5.4.

Wonder, Stevie. 1996. *Redemption Song*. Get on The Bus Music from and inspired by the motion picture CD. Interscope Records.

Woolery, George W. 1985. *Children's Television: The First Thirty-Five Years, 1946–1981. Pt. 2, Live, Film, and Tape Series*. Metuchen, NJ ; London: Scarecrow.

Young, Charles. 2022. 'Buffalo Soldiers'. *National Park Service*. 2022. https://www.nps.gov/chyo/learn/historyculture/buffalo-soldiers.htm#:~:text=American%20Plains%20Indians%20who%20fought,American%20regiments%20formed%20in%201866.

Index

Abu-Jamal, Mumia, 39
Adorno, Theodor, 94–95
Alleyne, Mike, 5, 15, 21, 88, 96, 97
Amazonics, 98
audiences, 1–6, 24, 26, 32, 45, 47–48, 52, 73, 83, 95, 103, 106

Balford, Henry, 61
Bangs, Lester, 6, 50–51, 62, 79, 104, 105
Bauman, Zygmunt, 99, 100, 101
Black Music, 47
Blanc Francard, Patrice, 76
BBC, 5, 11, 26, 33, 35, 39, 40, 62, 66, 84, 85, 104
Barker, Bingie, 80–83, 85, 103, 106
Billboard, 11, 46, 97
Blackburn, Tony, 32
Blackwell, Chris, 12, 50–51, 90, 92, 94, 95, 96
Bowen, Glenn A., 4, 45
Bowie, David, 2, 35, 110
Bordowitz, Hank, 63
Brackett, David, 43
Bradley, Lloyd, 27, 28, 31, 32
Bradshaw, Paul, 55, 91
Breakspeare, Cindy, 56–57
'Buffalo Soldier', 91–100
Buffalo Soldiers, 93, 94

cable television, 81, 83, 103, 104
Campbell, Horace, 67, 104
Caribbean News Network, 90
Carr, Patrick, 49
Cash, Johnny, 98
Catch A Fire, 15, 44, 48, 53, 96, 98
Chin, Earl, 80, 83
CIA, 56, 58, 98
code, 47–63;
coding tree, 45
Cohen, Mitchell, 56
Cohen, Stanley, 73
Coleman, Wanda, 38
college radio, 36, 38, 41
Commisso, Christina, 73
Concert Archives, 35, 59, 60, 98
Connolly, Mike, 33
Coral Gardens, 67
Crawdaddy, 11, 46
Creem, 46, 63
Crenshaw, Kimberle, 21
Crocker, Frank, 36, 41

Dalrymple, Henderson, 10
Davis, Stephen, 5, 12, 12, 50, 52, 59, 106
DBC, 28
Denselow, Robin, 7, 62, 84
digital, 3, 5, 24, 98, 99, 100, 105
Di Spurio, Laura, 25

Index

Discogs, 7, 29, 88, 101
document analysis, 6, 45
Dread, Mikey, 28, 31
Duppy, 87
'Duppy Conqueror', 87
Dylan, Bob, 49

Ebony, 45
Essence, 45
Essex University, 1
ethnography, 12, 17, 51
Everett, Kenny, 35
Everybody's Magazine, 60, 62, 63, 106
Exodus, 17, 48, 95, 96
exploratory research, 3

Facebook, 5, 99
Fraser, Dean, 98
Frith, Simon, 25, 47, 48, 65
folk devil/s – Cohen, 62, 73

Gambaccini, Paul, 26, 33, 35
Gauntlett, David, 43, 99
Gayle, Carl, 47, 48, 52, 105
Geertz, Clifford, 18, 28
Gilbert, Steve, 37, 38
Gillet, Charlie, 48
George, Nelson, 89
Gilroy, Paul, 5, 16, 21, 89, 99, 100
Golding, Johnny, 47
Goldman, Vivien, 5, 6, 15, 17, 18, 21, 28, 48, 50, 51, 57, 75, 105
gonzo journalism, 6, 7, 8, 51, 78, 80, 83
Gordon, Maxine, 33
Grant, Colin, 14, 26, 27, 28, 33, 36, 40, 104

Haile Selassie, 52, 54, 68, 77
Hall, Herman, 60, 62, 63, 81, 106
Hall, Stuart, 3, 4, 23, 66, 73, 104
Hajimichael, Mike, 3, 7, 22, 45, 46, 49, 57, 73, 82, 83
Hefner, Hugh, 48, 49
Holt, John, 32

Hope, Donna P., 53
Hope Road, 30, 57, 70, 71
Hoskyns, Barney, 8, 45, 103
Houston, Whitney, 2
Hussey, Dermot, 13, 28, 30, 31,67

Instagram, 100
'Iron Lion Zion', 15, 100
Irie FM, 27, 41
Island Records, 14, 15, 17, 33, 35, 36, 41, 44, 65, 88, 90, 91, 91, 94, 95, 103

Jackson, Michael, 2, 88, 99, 101
Jacobs, Curtis, 16, 17
JAD, 27
Jah Hammer Hi-Fi, 1
Jah Shaka, 5
Jagger, Mick, 49
JBC, 26, 28, 26, 28, 30, 39, 67
James, Marlon, 22, 58
Johnson, Richard, 30
Jones, Steve, 103
journalism, 6, 7, 11, 17, 48, 51, 54, 71, 73, 74, 81, 83, 103
Jurgensen, Joe, 9, 10, 12, 13

Kaya, 15
Kent, Nick, 47
King Sporty, 92–94
King, Jonathan, 32
Kornelis, Chris, 95, 96

Lee, Hermione, 10
Legend, 21, 88, 94, 95, 96, 97, 100, 106
Legend Remixed, 15
Lennon, John, 2
Longhurst, Brian, 5

Maeder, Jo, 36, 40, 41
mainstream/mainstreaming, 2, 5, 6, 26,28, 32, 33, 34, 35, 36, 37, 38, 39, 40, 41, 43, 45, 46, 47, 48, 49, 50, 57, 58, 61, 62, 74, 74, 83, 96, 97, 103, 105, 106
Manley, Michael, 51, 62

Index

Marcus, Griel, 48
Marley, Bob:
   academic writings, 14–17;
   assassination attempt, 17, 22, 50, 61, 66, 67, 75, 77, 79;
   biographies, 9–14;
   cancer, 30, 37, 39, 54, 56, 59–62, 98, 106;
   death, 1, 2, 5, 7, 9, 10, 12, 14, 15, 26, 31, 40, 54, 56, 59–62, 65, 66, 84, 85, 87, 88, 89, 97, 98, 100, 106;
   documentaries, 65, 66, 68–71, 98–99, 105;
   educational, 20, 22;
   family/personal life, 56–57, 100;
   language/xenoglossophobia, 6, 12, 13, 26, 40, 50–52, 62, 104;
   legacy, 60, 87–88, 90–91, 97–98, 100, 104;
   legal complexities, 89–90;
   mythologization/code, 55–56
   See also media; radio; television
Marley, Cedella Booker, 12, 9, 19, 22
Marley, Rita, 19, 22, 29, 56, 62, 90
Marre, Jeremey, 32, 40, 104
Masouri, John, 13, 14, 105
McKnight, Cathy, 11, 31
media, 2, 3, 4, 6, 43–64, 65, 75, 203, 104
Melody Maker, 21, 43, 46
Michael, George, 2
Midnight Raver, 8, 11, 30, 40, 58,
Millans, Anna, 76
Miss World 1974 (Cindy Breakspeare), 56–57
Morris, Dennis, 21
Morrow, Bruce, 75–76, 81, 83
Moskowitz, David V., 13
MTV, 65
Murray, Charles Shaar, 52, 53, 62

Nash, Johnny, 27
Needs, Kris, 6, 52, 104
Negus, George, 68–71, 79, 83, 98, 105
Negus, Keith, 14

New Musical Express (*NME*), 43, 46, 54, 61, 62
Noble, Gil, 7, 80, 81, 83, 106

Official Bob Marley website, 7, 99
One Love Peace Concert, 30, 51, 59, 63, 66, 75, 76
OnStage (TV show), 104

patwa/patois, 16, 8, 28, 35, 38, 40, 52, 78, 104
Peel, John, 25, 32, 33, 35, 40, 41, 43, 104
Perry, Lee, 87
Piepenbring, Dan, 10
Pine, Courtney, 98
Playboy, 4, 47, 48–49, 55, 106
Polygram, 90, 101
popular music, 25, 53, 54, 84, 88, 90, 91, 94, 95, 100
Presley, Elvis, 2, 88, 202
Presthold, Jeremy, 16, 21, 100
Prince, 2, 10

qualitative methods/research, 3, 9, 45

radio, 1, 2, 3, 4, 5, 6, 16, 23–43, 44, 46, 60, 62, 65, 75, 81, 103, 104
Rastafari, 11, 27, 38, 39, 41, 47, 52, 54, 57, 67, 68, 70, 71, 72, 80, 84, 89, 93, 104
Rastaphobia, 67, 104
Rather, Dan, 7, 68, 69, 70, 71, 75, 76, 79, 83, 98
Reading Evening Post, 11
'Redemption Song', 22, 67, 92, 98
Reel, Penny, 53, 62, 91
representation(s), 1, 3, 4, 10, 20, 23, 24, 44, 45, 61, 62, 73, 83, 84
Rinaldo, Sandie, 7, 71–73, 78, 79, 83, 103
RJR, 22, 27, 28
Robinson, Dave, 95, 96, 97
Rockers Television, 83
Rocks Backpages, 45

Rodigan, David, 2, 25, 28, 31, 33, 34, 35, 36, 40, 41
Rodney, Walter, 17, 22
Rolling Stone, 11, 12, 144, 46, 50, 51, 59
Rototom Festival, 100

Salewicz, Chris, 52, 92
San Siro Stadium, 35, 63
Seaga, Edward, 51, 61, 62, 84
Sims, Danny, 27, 36, 37
Silverton, Pete, 51, 52, 53
Sinclair, Ron, 28, 30, 31, 39
Smile Jamaica Concert, 58, 75
Sounds, 43, 46
Sounds Black, 82, 83
Spencer, Neil, 6, 43, 47, 54, 61, 62, 78, 105
Smash Hits, 55
Steffens, Roger, 5, 6, 9, 18, 21, 30, 36, 37, 52, 56, 59, 67, 69, 71, 92, 93, 94, 105
Strausser, Jay, 36, 39
'stringsing up', 32
Strummer, Joe, 98
Swenson, John, 59
Swing magazine, 47, 61

Taite, Dylan, 7, 77–78, 83, 106
Taylor, Don, 59
television, 1, 2, 3, 4, 6, 7, 29 35, 65–86, 93, 94, 103, 104, 105, 106
The Beat magazine, 29, 36
The Bob Marley Foundation, 20
The Boston Globe, 12
The Daily Gleaner, 49, 61, 62, 67
The Daily Mirror, 47, 56, 61
The Flamingos, 93
The Guardian, 47, 61, 84
The Marley Estate, 14, 41, 90, 93
The New York Times, 11, 12, 47, 106

The Old Grey Whistle Test, 66
The Ottawa Journal, 58
The Persuasions, 93
The Piglets, 32
The Wailers, 14, 15, 26, 30, 32, 33, 34, 36, 48, 53, 54, 66, 67, 88, 90, 96, 101, 106
Terrell, Tom, 55
TikTok, 91, 101
Tilley, Bruno, 94
Time Out, 21
Tobler, John, 11, 31, 35, 36, 40, 104
Top Gear (BBC), 32, 33
Torres, Dominique, 76
Tosh, Peter, 14, 29, 30, 51, 67, 87, 90, 91
Toynbee, Jason, 5, 14, 43
Trenchtown, 52, 68, 84
Twitter, 5

United Press International (*UPI*), 58
Universal Music Group (UMG), 90, 101

Vanity Fair, 36
Voice of the Sufferers, 40, 44

Wailer, Bunny, 14, 29, 30, 51, 67, 87, 90, 91
Wallace, Leonie, 20
Western, TJ, 74, 75, 76, 78, 82, 83
White, Timothy, 5, 11, 12, 13, 19, 41, 56, 59, 92
Williams, Richard, 48, 55, 56, 61
Williams, Tony, 28, 34
Williams, Winford, 104
Willoughby, Neville, 28–30, 31, 67
Windrush Generation, 32
Winehouse, Amy, 1
Wilson, Basil, 60, 62, 63, 81, 106
Wonder, Stevie, 37, 98

Zimbabwe Independence Celebrations Concert, 35, 45, 63, 96, 98

About the Author

Mike Hajimichael is an Associate Professor and the Head of the Communications Department at the University of Nicosia, Cyprus, where he has taught for the last two decades. Mike is also a performance poet, recording artist, DJ, radio host, and independent writer. In the last two decades, these experiences have impacted and enriched his writing and research which focuses on Reggae/Dub, media representation, protest songs, and critical textual analysis.

www.ingramcontent.com/pod-product-compliance
Lightning Source LLC
Chambersburg PA
CBHW061844300426
44115CB00013B/2501